About the Author

My name is Issy Hart, and I've been living with cerebral palsy for all of my life. I currently live in Oxfordshire with my family, and I started writing this book when I was seventeen years old. Growing up with cerebral palsy, there wasn't really a book out there that I could turn to for support so I didn't feel as alone as I did. I'm hoping this book can be that book for many other people living with cerebral palsy and other disabilities as well.

Cerebral Palsy and Me

Issy Hart

Cerebral Palsy and Me

Vanguard Press

A CIP catalogue record for this title is
available from the British Library.

ISBN 978 1 80016 844 2

*Vanguard Press is an imprint of
Pegasus Elliot Mackenzie Publishers Ltd.*
www.pegasuspublishers.com

First Published in 2023

**Vanguard Press
Sheraton House Castle Park
Cambridge England**

Printed & Bound in Great Britain

For nanny Jude.

"There's no word such as can't."

Thank you to my family for supporting me throughout my life, and the process of writing this book.

Contents

Introduction

I Have Always Wondered...

I have always wondered about something. It's actually kind of strange, as people do it all the time, but here goes. I've always wondered: what's it like to make a cup of tea and then carry it in one hand to wherever you want to drink it? Surely you have to have some kind of special skill, first of all, to make the cup of tea without accidently burning yourself on the kettle or with the boiling hot water in the kettle, and then having to carry it in one hand without spilling it and not getting burnt by the newly made tea? How do you actually do all of that whilst making a cup of tea? I've also always wondered what it's like to ride a two-wheeled bike without falling off. I'm talking about an adult riding a bike, not a child, because I'm sure, as children, we all fell off two-wheeled bikes all the time when we started to practise riding. But as an adult, when you have learnt to ride a bike, surely, you're still going to fall off or maybe you can't ride a bike at all? What I mean is, surely a bike with two wheels is an unbalanced bike, and how can you possibly ride an unbalanced bike? I still don't quite fully understand that bit.

I have also always wondered… Actually, I'm not going to keep going on about the many things that I've always wondered as I think we'd be here all night. It's 4:44 a.m. as I'm writing this, so that's why I say "night" instead of "day".

You see, I wonder about a lot of things that people simply do without any struggle in their day-to-day lives, such as riding a bike or making a cup of tea without spilling it. You are probably thinking, out of all of the things that I can wonder about in this world, why on earth do I wonder about those? What boring things they are to be wondering about, right? So, I'm going to tell you exactly why I sometimes wonder about these simple day-to-day tasks and even more such tasks. I can't do any of the tasks that I have mentioned here, because *it* won't let me. If I were to make a cup of tea and carry it, well, I would get as far as trying to lift an ordinary kettle and then it would probably go completely wrong from there. I wouldn't actually end up having a cup of tea because I would probably be going mad at not being able to lift the kettle and pour the scorching water from it into a cup, with my hand under the tap running cold water on where I burnt it from the scorching hot water, trying to make my hand feel and look better in some way. But carrying a hot cup of tea, well, that's quite another story. I won't go there. And as for riding a bike, well, I could probably get on a two-wheeled bike, but it wouldn't let me balance in order to be able to actually ride the bike and so I would fall off within the first five seconds of attempting to ride it.

Now, I've mentioned the word "it" a few times and have put "it" into the context of talking about a person, but when I'm using the word "it" to refer to what I'm talking about, I'm talking about a particular thing, a something. Something that has affected me and my life since the day I drew my first breath on entering this world. Something that makes me different from everyone else in a certain way. Something that restricts me in so many different ways. Something that anyone can get from birth, no matter what gender they are or who their parents and family are. Something that can have an impact on a whole family, even though it only physically affects one individual. Something that is a massive part of my life and has been for over seventeen years, nearly eighteen at this current point in time, and will continue to be for however long I live. That something is called cerebral palsy. It's a disability that affects an individual physically that is caused by brain damage, but it can change and have so many impacts and effects on a person's life straightaway, without anyone even knowing about it a minute before it becomes *something* for someone.

My name is Issy Hart, and I'm currently seventeen-years-old and living in Oxfordshire. I'm one of thousands of people worldwide living with cerebral palsy and fighting it every single day. I'm writing this book, hopefully, to try and give you all an insight into what it is like living with cerebral palsy.

How I Got Cerebral Palsy

On 30th January 2004, my twin brother and I were born. My brother was born before me, all healthy and crying, then forty minutes later I arrived. Unfortunately, it didn't go as planned. I wasn't breathing when I was born. The doctors said that, when I was still in the womb after my brother had arrived, my heart stopped and so I was starved of oxygen. This meant that I suffered brain damage due to a lack of oxygen. The doctors managed to resuscitate me immediately after my birth. I was then taken to the SCBU (special care baby unit) where I fought for my life. In total I spent three weeks in the SCBU and then went home when I was well enough.

I spent my first year going to doctor's appointments and seeing specialists, whilst everyone around me was trying to figure out what was wrong with me and why I wasn't developing like my twin brother. Questions were asked about why I wasn't reaching the milestones that he was reaching. Then, after my first birthday, I was diagnosed with cerebral palsy.

Chapter One

What is Cerebral Palsy... To Me?

If you were to ask a doctor or a nurse or any kind of medical specialist what cerebral palsy is, they'd probably describe it as a neurological condition that affects an individual physically. It means that they can't function physically like everyone else can and it's normally caused by brain damage. This is in fact true, in medical terms anyway, but it isn't what cerebral palsy is to me.

You see, I don't view cerebral palsy as a neurological condition that affects me physically; I've probably never seen it that way in all my seventeen years of living with it. Sure, I know the medical conditions that come with it, as I've had to endure them all, but I don't, and never will, see it that way. What cerebral palsy is to me isn't a neurological condition — it's a neurological pain up the backside.

It's falling over nothing in the middle of the street; it's waking up in the middle of the night in agony from the leg cramps that have occurred over the past few hours while you've been asleep; it's getting looked at, no, stared at by strangers when you're in a shop; it's feeling worthless simply because you're different; it's wishing you could be like everyone else but also knowing that it will never go away. It's a whole range of different things — these are just a very few of the things that come from living with cerebral palsy. I think we would be here for a while if I were to list them all!

I've lived with cerebral palsy pretty much from the day I was born, and I get asked all the time: What is it like living with cerebral palsy? To be honest with you, I can never answer that question, and the reason why is that I've never lived without cerebral palsy. I can't compare what it's like to live with cerebral palsy and what it's like to live without cerebral palsy, so I simply can't answer that question. However, so that people can get a better understanding of what it's like to live with cerebral palsy, I can describe it as being like having weights on you 24/7, wherever you go or whatever you do. Those weights are always with you, trying to drag you down and making whatever you do a little bit harder. That's probably the best way I can describe it.

You see, other people are lucky, they don't have to live life feeling like they are carrying these weights and they probably find doing the normal day-to-day things that are done in life a lot easier than I do. They probably don't have to think about all the risks and the 'what if's' when they do normal daily jobs and just get on with doing them without giving it a second thought. They probably don't have to worry about the footwear that would be most sensible for walking down the street, just in case they fall over, nor to worry about ordering a drink with a lid on it in case they spill it. I bet they don't even think of such things even once a day while they're living their normal lives.

For me, living with cerebral palsy means worrying about these things on a daily basis. Being able to live a carefree life where I don't have to worry about little things such as I've mentioned above would be an absolute dream for me and is something I envy every day. Being able to live a life without setbacks is the life I want but unfortunately I will never have the privilege of living and experiencing. I see people every day living normally without any barriers getting in their way and just getting on with life. Having cerebral palsy means that I can't do that; no matter what I do or where I go, there will always be barriers in my way, always trying to stop me from achieving what I want to achieve.

Everything I do in life has to revolve around my disability. No matter how big or small an activity is, cerebral palsy has to be at the centre of everything I do most of the time. This is irritating because I'm only seventeen-years-old; I've got my whole life ahead of me, and there are loads of things I want to do in this life that I may never be able to do, either because they are

18

too physically demanding for me or because I may need extra support to do them and that support may not be available to me at that time for some reason. Knowing that these barriers may disrupt my dreams is heartbreaking. This is one thing that's going to be hard for me to accept as I grow older and see all my friends and siblings going out into the big wide world and living carefree lives — because I'm never going to be able to do that. I'm never going to be able to go out there and live a carefree life like they can, because, for me, there's always planning that has to be done and stuff that has to be put in place before I can even dream of doing what I'd like to do — even if I'm going to be able to do those things at all.

As an individual, you're expected to go through a normal, healthy childhood and then morph into a moody teenager, hanging out in the fields at night with their friends, and then go to university and get a degree; and then meet someone, fall in love with them, get married and have children and live happily ever after. That's the stereotypical view of life.

As a person with cerebral palsy, this stereotypical view of life can sometimes make me really angry. How can you simply expect a child to be born healthy and then go through childhood as a healthy child, when not all children are born that way? How can you expect a teenager to go and hang out with their friends when some teenagers are 'different', and simply struggle to make friends because no one understands why they are like they are and then, because of that, people don't want to be friends with them? How can you expect someone to go to university and then meet someone, get married and have children, when that may not be possible for them for many different reasons? Life isn't always like that, especially not for people like me living with cerebral palsy and for people with any other disability.

It's really hard for me to try and imagine the future I want for myself, because the future I want for myself is weirdly exactly like the stereotypical view of how an individual should live their life that I get angry about. I want to go to university; I want to get married and have children; but I don't expect myself to achieve those things in life, simply because I have cerebral palsy. I've already been through a childhood that's different to most people's childhoods, and as a teenager, I've lived a life that is far from being a typical teenager's life. In my eyes, therefore, why would my adulthood be 'normal' and how I want it to be, when my life so far has not been what I've wanted it to be or the kind of life you'd expect a normal person to live?

Because I have cerebral palsy, I often think about the opposite of what I want my life to be like, so I won't get disappointed if it turns out to be not what I wanted it to be. Deep down, I know I shouldn't think like that, and people often tell me to think of the positives. Sometimes I wonder how can I think of the positives? What's so positive about living with a disability? But then, at other times, I do think of the positives. I often wonder what my life would've been like if I didn't have cerebral palsy. To be honest with you, if I didn't have cerebral palsy, I probably wouldn't have come as far as I have done in life up until now, because my disability makes me appreciate the little things in life and how precious life is; so I guess that's an advantage of living with a disability.

I see myself as a regular person who has no barriers to confront and who can do whatever they want to do. To the outside world, however, I'm a disabled person who can't do what everyone else can do and is a bit more dependent on others. I guess I find it hard when people see me this way, because I don't want to be seen this way. I want people to see me how I see myself. Sometimes, because of this, I've received negative comments from people, often from people around my age. Most of these comments are made behind my back, but some are made to my face. When I hear a negative comment aimed at my disability, sometimes it makes me think that having a disability is a bad thing.

When I was at primary school, a lot of negative comments were made about me, which sometimes resulted in me getting bullied. In fact, this would happen all the time: kids would make nasty comments behind my back or to my face, usually aimed at my disability. This was because they simply didn't understand why I was different and so, to deal with it, they would bully me about being disabled. I understand now that they probably didn't know how to be friendly, in the same way as they were with all the other classmates, with a classmate who had a disability. But at the time, it had a huge impact on me, and from then on, I've always seen my disability as a negative — actually, until quite recently. Now that I've grown up, however, people of my age have a better understanding and so, luckily, I don't experience bullying any more.

But there are still people out there who make negative comments to try and bring me down and sometimes they succeed, because their comments do get to me. But then, at other times, I think that I can't change myself so, if they don't like who I am, it's their problem.

Cerebral palsy is usually seen as a negative by most people, and even I still see it as a negative sometimes, but maybe if it wasn't seen as such a negative then people living with it wouldn't feel so different. I've always felt different because I'm disabled, and sometimes, I don't like being different, but then at other times I do. When I don't like feeling different, to make myself feel better, I look at all the things that I've achieved having cerebral palsy. That makes me feel proud of myself, because having cerebral palsy is hard and I wasn't expected to achieve as much as I've achieved to this very day. So I guess cerebral palsy is a good thing, mainly because of that reason, and because of it, I have a better outlook on life than I would have done a year ago, two years ago or even ten years ago.

Cerebral palsy is a lot of things to a lot of people and for me it's the same. But for me, I guess it's a part of me and who I am — I wouldn't be who I am today without it.

Chapter Two

Day-to-Day Life
Living with a Disability

$\mathcal{E}$very day I wake up like any other ordinary teenager would, have breakfast and get ready to start the day. It's just that there's a tiny difference which is my disability and everything I do in my day-to-day life sometimes has to revolve around my disability.

For instance, I need to take precautions with daily activities, such as walking to my friend's house. I could fall over and hurt myself or, while carrying a hot drink, I could lose my balance or have a muscle spasm and spill the drink all over myself, which would burn me. It's day-to-day activities like these I need to take my time doing and I need to be careful whilst doing them.

As I've said, people have asked me in the past about what it's like living with cerebral palsy, and to be honest, that's a really hard question to answer. I don't know what it's like to live life without a disability as I've been disabled since birth, so I can't compare what it's like living with a disability to what it's like living without a disability. Another way that I like to describe it is to say it's like wearing heavy weights all the time that restrict you from doing certain things. Your muscles are constantly aching, and your fingers have hardly any grip. I have to put twice as much effort into doing things as everyone else around me.

There are various normal day-to-day exercises that people take for granted. Unfortunately, in some cases I can't do them. I find it difficult to ask for help when I'm doing these types of jobs because, to be honest, I want to be fully independent and feel that asking for help with certain things suggests I can't be independent. That sucks. Especially when buttoning up a school shirt or making a hot meal for myself. These can take me a lot of time to do, or I'll cause a mess. It's really hard and frustrating, and when I was younger, I would often avoid asking for help or assistance as I didn't want to be seen as a failure.

No matter how stubborn I was in not asking for help, over the years I've learnt that, if I want to get on with my day-to-day life, I'd rather ask for help than just sit there and lose time struggling with doing up shirt buttons or tying up shoelaces. By asking for help and accepting my limits, I get the shirt sorted and the shoelaces tied up and then I can get on with whatever I have planned. It gives me more time to do and enjoy the good stuff in life.

I know that this will probably have to happen for the rest of my life when doing certain exercises. The reality is that I can't be independent in all of the activities that my siblings or friends are able to do in their lives. There are times when I watch my parents cook meals or make hot drinks and I ask myself: how can they do that? How can they make a hot meal or a hot drink without burning themselves or spilling anything? And that amazes me. I would love to be able to do simple jobs like these without putting myself at risk.

It's frustrating because I can't do these jobs yet and I know that, when I'm eventually going to be able to do them, I will have to do them differently to the way my parents or my siblings do them and I'll need special equipment to help me out. This isn't how I want to come across to others when I'm doing these jobs. I want to use normal cooking tools like the rest of my family, and I want to be able to carry a cup of tea in one hand, but I need to accept that I won't be able to do such jobs as those.

But even though there are things I can't do I make the most out of the normal day-to-day stuff that I can do and have achieved in my life so far. This includes making myself a bowl of cereal, brushing my teeth, and getting myself showered and dressed without buttons being involved. I know that these are probably really small things for people without disabilities who find it really easy to carry out day-to-day chores like brushing their teeth, but for me, I cherish the fact that I can be fully independent when carrying out such day-to-day activities.

The reason I feel this way is because, when I was first diagnosed with cerebral palsy, my parents were told by doctors and specialists that I may never be able to do anything for myself. I can't imagine a life like that now, and the fact that I can brush my teeth and get myself ready in the morning is down to choosing never to give up.

I feel blessed that I'm able to walk and talk and be partly independent and do things for myself. Hopefully I'll be able to carry out all those activities I have achieved so far for the rest of my life — and that's what gets me up in the mornings. The fact that there are people out there who can't do anything for themselves because they have disabilities that are more severe than mine makes me realise that I am quite fortunate. For example, there were jobs that I used to struggle with doing for myself such as managing personal hygiene. I couldn't clean myself properly and I never thought I'd be able to do it; and that thought brought me down. But now I can wash myself and look after my personal hygiene, and this gives me hope that I will achieve more in the foreseeable future. I see myself as kind of lucky because of this.

One other thing I like to do and achieve is to be like any other girl of my age. I like to go shopping. I like to do my makeup — why not? — even though I learnt to do makeup later than other girls my age. But at the back of my mind, I know that there are differences for me. I have to go to doctor's appointments and attend physio and speech therapy sessions which can sometimes mean that my life has to revolve around them. There are days when my friends ask me to meet up and I can't because I may have a doctor's appointment that day.

When I do meet up with my friends, they need to make certain allowances for me and have to work around my disability, as I can't do all the stuff they can do. This can be tiring for me because I don't have as much energy as them. At first, it made me feel guilty because, every time we met up, my disability would always be front of mind. This means we can't undertake certain activities when we're together and some of the activities have to revolve around me and whether I can do them or not.

I've had friends in the past who couldn't accept that being friends with me might be stopping them from what they wanted to do when they were hanging out with me. Because of this they walked away and never spoke to me again and that hurt, because I don't want my disability to put people off from getting to know me. But over the years, I've learnt not to feel guilty about something that I can't help and know that real friends will stand by me and will be willing to make allowances so that we can hang out together.

There are also other struggles and differences from other people, for example, your parents worrying about you when you go out by yourself; they worry about you more than they do about your siblings when they go out. This can be annoying at times because I want my parents to be able to treat me as an equal with my siblings. But I also understand that my disability makes me more vulnerable and I can't do everything in the same way as my siblings because, as I've said, I'm at more risk of falling over and hurting myself. But I've learnt how to make it easier for myself when I'm out shopping, doing stuff in public and getting around places, so that my parents don't worry about me as much.

I have introduced safer adjustments, such as taking the lift instead of the stairs, holding onto someone's arm when I'm tired, and walking in public, not rushing to get somewhere, to reduce the risk of me falling over. Through all these precautions I'm taking, I'm reducing risk to myself and making sure I'm safe when shopping or just being out in public and generally having a good time with whoever I'm with. This is a bit of a relief for my parents when I'm with them, as it means they don't have to be quite as on edge as if I weren't taking the precautions.

When I'm out in public on my own or with friends, it's not just taking extra precautions that is a struggle for me. There's a lot more. When I'm out in public, I get stared at, once at least, when I'm shopping or eating in a restaurant, enjoying myself and forgetting that I have a disability. Sometimes I don't even notice this, but when I do, it really annoys me (especially when an adult stares). It's rude to stare at someone, but then I know I stand out from everyone else and that someone has realised I'm 'different' and that's upsetting because I want to fit in. I don't want to be seen for my disability; I want to be seen as a normal person who's going about their day-to-day life and it reminds me that I have a disability and then I can't forget about it. I don't want to be looked at for my disability and yet sometimes it makes me feel like I'm not part of society because I'm disabled and others see me as disabled.

I also struggle communicating with members of the public, when I have to ask a stranger where something is, or when I'm paying in a shop and have a problem. It's not the people whom I ask for directions or something like that who are the problem, it's my voice and getting people to understand what I'm saying to them, because my cerebral palsy affects my voice.

I'm used to my family and friends understanding what I'm saying really well, and I hardly have to repeat myself so, when I'm talking to a stranger, repeating myself over and over again sometimes to try and make sure they understand me can occasionally get really irritating. I used to avoid talking to strangers for this reason and couldn't really be arsed to repeat myself because I was embarrassed by my voice. So, when I was paying at the till for something, I would say as little as possible to the person serving me or, when I was lost in a shopping centre, I would try and find my own way around rather than asking strangers for directions.

But then, I learnt that you have to do things you don't want to do, to get farther along in life, and now I don't hesitate to ask somebody for directions when I'm lost, because otherwise I would get nowhere. There are times when I have to accept that I'm going to have to repeat myself, but that's OK. I'd rather repeat myself to make someone understand what I'm asking for, rather than getting nowhere in what I'm trying to do or where I'm trying to go. I'm less embarrassed about my voice than I used to be.

And there are some things I've just begun doing that I should have been able to do at an earlier age, such as getting on the bus on my own, or cooking myself microwave meals. These little tasks have taken me longer to do than they should have done. This is partly because of my disability, but also because I'm scared of what will happen if something goes wrong or whether I'll be able to do it or if I don't have the courage to do it.

I remember getting on the bus for the first time on my own at sixteen years old and being frightened of doing it. I think it was just nerves and that's totally normal because, when people do certain things for the first time, it is scary, even if they don't have a disability. Succeeding in these tasks with a disability is more challenging, but once I was on the bus, the nerves just went, and I was really proud of myself for taking a bus ride for the first time in my life. It was a step towards a bit more independence. People may think it's another little thing again, but it's a big thing to me because I envy those who enjoy a fully independent life and getting the bus or making food for myself is me being independent, which I love to be in day-to-day life.

Day-to-day life with a disability is hard. Some days I'm happy, some days I'm angry, some days I'm sad, some days I get frustrated with myself when I can't do certain things, and some days, I just don't want to get out of bed... But I never give up, I choose to carry on, no matter how hard it is. There are setbacks, there are all kinds of difficulties that disability brings, but there are also a lot of privileges, and over the years, I've learnt to appreciate what I *can* do rather than dwell on what I *can't* do. There was a time when the doctors said it would be nearly impossible for me to achieve all the things I can do now. When I do achieve new things, I've also learnt to celebrate them, whether it's a big thing or a little thing. I'm proud of what I have achieved in my life so far and I'm looking forward to what I'm going to achieve in the future.

Chapter Three

How Living with a Disability is Viewed in Society

Disabled. Dis-abled. "Dis" and then "abled". I absolutely hate that word sometimes. I've never really noticed the context behind that word, and to me, it's always been a regular word just like any other word in the dictionary — I've never really looked into it properly. However, as I've got older and developed a better understanding of life in general and everything that it entails, quite recently the word 'disabled' has stood out a lot more for me.

To me, the word "disabled" nowadays means that an individual isn't able to do anything at all for themselves or anyone else and is simply useless for that reason, which in fact isn't true at all. Just because I'm disabled and have a disability doesn't mean that I'm useless and can't do anything for myself. It may seem weird to some people, but someone who is disabled may still walk and talk and do stuff for themselves and even for other people. It isn't impossible for a disabled person to do things just because they have a disability.

Living in a society where the majority of people aren't disabled, I feel as though having a disability or being disabled is still frowned upon to this day. And do you know what? I blame other generations for that. Mike and the Mechanics created a song called "The Living Years", which was in fact my nan's favourite song. The opening line of that song is "Every generation blames the one before", and I feel that line is so true when it's applied to how being disabled is seen; that's the way I see it, anyway. I blame the generation before, and the one before that, and then the one before that, for how disability is seen in society today.

Many years ago — or many generations ago to continue with what I said above — being disabled was seen as a bad thing. If you were disabled, then it meant that you were seen negatively by everyone else. You were treated differently to others, and you were even treated badly sometimes, well most of the time, for being disabled. As an individual living with a disability, I've experienced all of these things but less than I would've done if I had been born into a previous generation. I can't imagine what it must've been like for people who were disabled and living in the 1930s. Despite the changes in perception over time, I've still been treated badly, my disability has still been seen as a negative thing and I also get treated differently sometimes. This is what I expect to live with for the rest of my life.

Maybe if those earlier generations had changed the way being disabled and having a disability was seen and had made it out to be less of a negative thing, then maybe I wouldn't have had to experience the negatives or continue to experience them at times in my life. As I am disabled, even though I see myself as being the same as everyone else, I always expect to be treated differently to the way everyone else is treated. This is because, for the majority of my life, I've always been treated differently by those around me. I ask myself what might change in the future, so that I get treated exactly like everyone else?

Sometimes I don't mind it, as I understand that I am different in a way, and I can't do as much or the same things as others and so I need to be treated differently. But at other times, when there's been no need for me to be treated differently, it's been really frustrating to have to come to terms with and accept the way I've been treated. I'm human. I have a brain. I have a heart. I have everything that everyone else has got, so why is there a need for me to be treated differently to the way my friends are treated or the way my classmates are treated?

Sometimes, when I am treated differently for no apparent reason at all, I just want to scream, because I want people to know that I'm not expecting to be treated differently, I'm not expecting any kind of special treatment just because I'm disabled. I want to be like everyone else, I want to be seen like everyone else, I am technically like everyone else. Trying to get myself to be seen that way can be frustrating and upsetting at times because, no matter how hard I try to fit in with everyone else, I'm always going to stand out; wherever I go in life there's always going to be someone who sees me as different.

As a society, we don't really recognise differences in a good way, especially when it comes to being disabled. Your disability isn't seen as a good thing, and I know it's not a good thing. But then, sometimes, it's like you're not being seen as a 'good thing' because you're disabled, and that's because people have been taught to think that way by generations before them. I sometimes wonder what it would be like if disabled people were actually seen as normal. Normal. Another word I hate. What the heck is normal? In society, there is such a thing as "normal", but because I'm disabled and I walk funny and talk funny, I feel as though I don't fit within the "normal" category, as shown by the way I've been treated during my life to date.

One of the many things that I've had to face as a disabled person is getting stared at in the street. Because disability isn't seen as normal in society, and in my eyes, has never been seen as normal, when you're a person living with a disability, being stared at is normal, whether I'm going out shopping or I'm out for dinner or I'm walking to a bus stop. I expect to get stared at, at least once when I'm doing ordinary things.

Usually, it's children who stare, and when I was a child myself and another child would stare at me, it used to really upset me, because I felt as though they were judging me. But now I'm older, I understand why children stare. They're just trying to figure out why I am the way I am because, at that age, children haven't learnt everything about the world yet; they're still learning and trying to fully understand everything that goes on around them. So, it doesn't affect me as much any more when children stare because, as I see it, they are learning from staring, if that makes sense.

However, when adults stare at me, that's when I get offended, and this is why. First of all, as adults, we know that staring comes across as rude, as it could make someone feel very uncomfortable. I know this because I've experienced the feeling myself. But then, because adults understand that staring is rude, I don't understand why I still get stares from adults. But then again, it goes back to how being disabled was perceived generations ago which enables it to be seen the way it's seen today. I guess when an adult stares at me, they're staring because they don't see disabled people as "normal" people, and as people, when we see something that doesn't appear "normal" to us, our first reaction is to stare. But in my eyes, adults should know better and should know not to stare, whether something appears normal to them or not. Also, being stared at makes me feel all kinds of different things.

When I'm being stared at, I feel uncomfortable. I feel as if I'm being judged, but in this case by an adult and not a child staring at me. It's as though they're judging me on how I walk or how I talk or how I do certain things. And then I start to question myself. Am I doing this right? Is it obvious that I have a disability? Even down to asking myself whether I should hide my disability or not. I ask myself these things because I don't like feeling uncomfortable and I absolutely hate that feeling.

Of all the questions I ask myself, the one that gets to me most is "Should I hide my disability?" because I honestly feel as though I have to do that, to try and make myself look 'normal' so that I don't get stared at any more. But I shouldn't have to do that because, to me, if I did that, then it would be as if I'm hiding myself and I'm not being myself, just so that I don't get stared at any more. I hate getting stared at in general, but I'm not changing myself to look less disabled, because that's not the way to deal with situations like this.

I think that, if we could change how the world sees disabled people, the world would definitely be a better place for people like me. Thousands of people living with cerebral palsy and all kinds of other disabilities wouldn't experience situations such as being stared at when they're going about their day-to-day lives or all the terrible ways society treats disabled people, including bullying and abuse. Luckily, I have experienced very little bullying and abuse due to being disabled, in my teenage years, and have really only received stares and maybe a few sniggers. What really upsets me, though, are the stories I've heard of people living with all kinds of disabilities who experience bullying and all kinds of horrible treatment in their daily lives. As a person living with a disability, this makes me angry and heartbroken at the same time.

Why? Why do people living with disabilities get targeted with this type of abuse? It isn't fair, they haven't done anything to deserve this at all. Knowing that people with disabilities are experiencing things in this way doesn't make me very hopeful that society will change in the way disability is seen in the future. Will I experience any of these things in the future because I'm disabled? This really frightens me. I want there to be change, so that being disabled isn't seen as such a negative thing, but as a society, we need to make that change, we can't keep treating disabled people like this. I think it so unfair that disabilities have been around for years and years yet still, to this day, being disabled is seen in a negative way when it shouldn't be; it should be celebrated instead of being reviled.

As an individual who experienced bullying when a child and having been treated differently all my life, I can sit here and say that how a disability is seen needs to change so that, in society, disabled people are seen as real people instead of as beings who are somehow alien to the world.

I don't want to be seen as different, I don't want to be treated like a baby, I don't want to be stared at in the street. I just want to be seen the way everyone else is seen and treated the way everyone else is treated. We don't have to follow past generations in how we see things, we can change how we see things so that, in future generations, people living with disabilities won't have to experience the negative things that I have experienced as someone living with a disability and that thousands of people around the world living with disabilities experience. I hope that, one day, we can all live in a world where living with a disability isn't seen as such a bad thing and differences are celebrated a lot more.

Chapter Four

Fitting In

There's a quote that reads: "Why fit in when you were born to stand out?" I've never really taken any notice of this quote until quite recently, and now I actually get the meaning behind the quote. Why would you want to fit in and be like everyone else, when you were born to stand out and be your own self? I think, as a society, we all want to fit in with one another and to be seen as exactly the same as everyone else, but the truth is that everyone is different, no one is the same as the next person. As for me, I am definitely not the same as everyone else for many reasons, but in this instance, because I have cerebral palsy which most people around me don't have. That's the main thing that makes me different. I guess you could say it makes me one of a kind in a way. I don't mind being different or however you prefer to term it, but growing up with a disability, it hasn't always been like that.

I used to hate being different from everyone else, I used to hate not being seen like everyone else, and not being acknowledged in the same way as everyone else was, which then led me to hate my disability as well. I didn't like the fact that I "stood out". I wanted to be like everyone else, and no matter what, I was going to make that happen and do everything I possibly could to fit in. I think every child who's going into their teens feels this pressure to be like everyone else, but for me, I felt extra pressure because I had a disability as well.

I want to tell you a bit about what I did to try and fit in. I hope that, if you're a teenager who has a disability and you're in the same shoes I was in and you're desperate to fit in, you can take something — anything in fact — away from what I'm about to tell you.

When I was ten years old, I realised I was different from everyone else, and that new realisation had a really negative impact on how I saw myself. Most of the first ten years of my life were spent with me pretty much despising my disability, which then meant me despising myself and the person I was. I hated how I walked and I hated the sound of my own voice; it used to go as far as blocking my ears every time I listened to a video of myself talking. I hated everything about myself. So, at the age of ten, filled with self-hate, and in an effort to fix it somehow by changing myself, I started wanting to be like everyone else.

It started off with me asking my mum to buy me some new clothes that I wanted for Christmas, and so she did. But I didn't actually want the clothes because I liked them or thought that they would suit me; I wanted them because all the other girls in my year were wearing the exact same clothes, or similar clothes, outside school or on non-school uniform days. That's why I wanted them. In my eyes, this was the very first step in trying to hide my disability. And so, by having these clothes and new shoes as well sometimes, this very first step towards being like everyone else was being fulfilled.

However, when it came to wearing these clothes on non-school uniform days, when all the other children could see how I was, step one had failed. I remember going in on one of these non-school uniform days, wearing similar, if not the same clothes as the other children would wear — the girls especially, and being disappointed because, even though I looked the same as everyone else, I still wasn't seen as being the same as all the other children. I was still stared at, I still had very few friends, I was still seen as "the disabled girl". Even though I had changed everything outwardly about myself, how I was seen by my classmates didn't change at all.

I was so angry that it hadn't worked, that I still didn't fit in with everyone else around me, so I felt even worse about myself than before. Was there anything that I could do to hide my disability? This question stuck with me from my last years of primary school all the way to when I started secondary school. When I first went to secondary school, I still had the same goal to fit in and hide my disability and put even more pressure on myself to do that. This time, not only would I try and wear the same clothes as everyone else, I would also start wearing makeup. But it wasn't just my style that I changed. You see, the saddest part for me wasn't just changing what I wore, it was changing my personality to fit in with everyone else's personality.

When I was at primary school, I never used to swear, not even in my home life. I was too scared to do so. I never heard swearing at primary school, but when I went to secondary school, that was a different story. I would hear all kinds of swear words when I was walking the corridors of secondary school, which I expected because older kids do swear. Most of the time, though, I would hear other students who were the same age as me swear as well. Before I went to secondary school, I could never imagine myself swearing as it just wasn't me, I didn't want to swear, I didn't feel the need to. But at this stage of my life, where all I wanted to do was hide my disability and fit in and everyone else around me at school was swearing, in order to fit in, I started swearing as well.

To me, this was a new way of trying to fit in, as wearing the same styles as everyone else didn't exactly work as well as I'd hoped it would. For a girl who never used to swear at all before this point in her life, this was quite a big personality change. Every sentence I spoke to my peers or friends had at least one swear word in it. I saw it as cool because, from my point of view, swearing hid my disability. Every time I swore, I saw it as a bit more of my disability being hidden away from the world, which was the effect I wanted. I wanted to hide my disability, and if I looked cool by swearing, then no one could see my disability.

But it didn't have that effect at all. All it did was make me look rude and stupid as I was only eleven years old at the time. It must've done. No matter how many times I swore, it didn't change how I felt about myself, I still hated myself for being disabled, and in particular, it didn't hide my disability at all. I still felt like an outsider and other students still treated me differently to the way everyone else was treated. Yeah, I got a few people to laugh with me and talk to me, but this was probably because it must have been fascinating to see a disabled person like me swear, or maybe they saw a bit more of an individual who was like them and swearing broke down this barrier for them. I don't know the answer to this. But I didn't gain a whole load of new friends which is what I wanted to happen. Yet again, this disappointed me, as I didn't get the reaction I was hoping for from other people.

Going into secondary school, I did feel this peer pressure to look normal, but what I didn't realise was that I looked fine, I was just disabled. But because I was disabled, I didn't think I looked normal at all. So I guess that's why I changed my style and my personality, to be completely "normal" like everyone else because, in my eyes, I wasn't normal. I hated that. Every time I looked at myself in the mirror, I saw nothing good about myself at all. I saw no positives when I looked at myself. All I saw was an ugly, disabled mess. I think that, knowing you're seen as different from the rest of the world because of the way you've been treated in society, made me feel all these different, negative emotions towards myself. For me, feeling like an outsider was one of the loneliest feelings in the world.

I'd been seen differently, I'd been treated differently, I'd been bullied, I'd been looked at in the street or wherever I went for so long that, when I was coming towards the end of secondary school, after years of trying to change myself multiple times in order to fit in and change all the things I'd been experiencing for years, I had just had enough. I felt so angry that, no matter what I did, I could never seem to fit in anywhere and that really bothered me. In my eyes, I was the problem, and this was why I wasn't seen as "normal" like everyone else.

I had tried everything: from changing what I wore and wearing makeup to changing my personality, even trying to change how I walked and talked when I was at school or out and about, so that people didn't recognise I had a disability. None of that had worked at all. I guess my one main goal, as I was going through my teens and through secondary school, was to fit in; all my other goals and dreams were pushed to one side and because I didn't quite achieve this goal, I felt so angry and disheartened. After years of asking myself whether, if I did this or wore that, then just maybe I would be seen as 'normal' for once, I simply didn't see the point of this any more.

I couldn't be bothered going through the rest of my life being seen as different and so I just wanted to give up. I was drained by trying to make myself a completely different person physically to what I had been before I entered my teens and before I had this immense urge to fit in. I had just had enough of standing out. Going through this stage of my life, I hadn't put my feelings or myself first, because I was too focussed on trying to fit in. So, because of that, I had overlooked my mental health.

You see, it doesn't matter how you look or what you do in order to get other people's approval, it's how you feel in general and towards yourself that really matters. I think, for me, coming towards the end of my teens and looking back, I never really saw that; how I felt wasn't my priority and how I was seen by others was.

Nowadays, I don't care how I'm seen by others or whether I fit in or not. Sure, I still want to keep up with the latest fashion trends for my age group, but I'm not as desperate about it now as I was back then when I was at school. Nowadays, the way I see it is that you can't really expect anyone to accept you for who you are until you accept yourself. Every time I feel low about myself and question myself and how I look, I always remind myself of this.

Was I happy years ago trying to make myself fit in? No. Now, I realise that standing out is a lot better than fitting in and I think that needs to be celebrated more than it is, so that fewer people, disabled or not, feel as much pressure to fit in. So, if you're reading this and you're in a position that's similar to how I was, please realise your worth and love yourself for who you are and not for what other people may want you to be. Wear whatever you want and that you feel comfortable in, be yourself everywhere you go, don't change for anyone. Be yourself, it doesn't matter if you fit in or not. Sometimes you were born to stand out.

Chapter Five

What Did You Take for Granted Today?

What did you take for granted today? Was it walking up the stairs? Was it writing a reminder for your loved one on a piece of paper? Was it driving a car? Was it just simply taking a walk down the street? You see, we all take the things I've listed here for granted, don't we? There's no denying it. When we carry out normal day-to-day activities, we never give them a second thought. If you're making a meal or something, maybe you think about how starving you are and how you can't wait to wolf down that sandwich you're preparing. Well, I do anyway because I'm a bit of a pig.

But we never think about how lucky we are to be able to do daily jobs, because we do them every day and it's the norm for everyone. But what if you were robbed of the ability to carry out day-to-day activities in your normal life and you couldn't do anything, either for yourself or anyone else? How would you feel? The unfortunate thing is that this is the reality for some people. Some people don't have the privilege of being able to do all the things that most of us do in life, and it's because they have some kind of barrier that holds them back.

As a girl with a disability, I have some kind of understanding of what it's like not being able to do all the things that your friends and family can do. Although I am privileged in being able to do most things, I am not sufficiently privileged that I can do everything. So I can't even begin to imagine what it must be like for people out there who are living with more severe disabilities than I have and who are unable to do anything at all for themselves. Being able to do most things but being unable to do every single thing is hard enough for me, let alone not being able to do anything.

I've always felt lucky with my disability, as I can undertake the basics in life like most people can, such as walking, talking and writing. To me, that's better than not being able to do anything, but learning to be able to carry out the basics in life has been a bit of a rocky road for me. Everything I do, everything I have achieved in my life has had its ups and downs. There's always been a barrier in front of me, trying to stop me from achieving what I want to achieve, no matter how big or small the thing that I want to achieve is — that barrier has always been there. You can't remove it, you can't knock it down, it's there and it isn't going anywhere. You just have to live with it. Sometimes it's really irritating, and you just want to scream whilst wanting to physically kick the barrier down, other times you don't mind it. But most of the time I just get on with it as if that barrier wasn't there, because I've learnt to live with it, and I'm used to it by now.

However, it has never stopped me from wondering what life is like for people who don't have to worry about a barrier in front of them and who can do whatever they like without any barriers holding them back. For them it must be like floating wherever they go, without any weight holding them back at all. Living life without any limits or barriers would be an absolute dream and feeling like I'm floating instead of feeling like there's a weight holding me down would be amazing. Not a day goes by when I don't imagine what life would be like without a disability. Don't get me wrong, I wouldn't change my disability for the world as it's what makes me who I am, but it still doesn't stop me wondering what it would be like if I weren't disabled.

I think about this all the time. I think about what it would be like to make myself a cup of tea and be able to carry it around with me, so that I can sip it wherever and whenever I want to, instead of having to bend right down to the height of the table it's on and then drink it slowly and steadily or drink it with a straw — a bright pink one in fact. I hate drinking tea from a bright pink straw. First, it burns your mouth and second, it's bright pink. That must attract a whole lot of attention! But then, at least people know which cup of tea is mine and I won't get anybody accidentally drinking it and saying, "Oh, sorry, I got confused and thought it was mine". The bright pink straw is like a name tag in a way: ISSY'S TEA, DON'T TOUCH OR DRINK FROM IT. On a serious note, though, how many of you have to drink your cup of tea from a straw because you can't pick it up physically and lift it to your mouth? If there were no straw, by the time it reached your mouth, most of it would either be spilt down you or spilt on the floor.

You probably wouldn't even associate a cup of tea with a straw as it's not normal to drink a cup of tea from a straw. I never see people do this in cafes or wherever else. But living with a disability means doing things differently from others, and for me, drinking a cup of tea with a straw is one of these different things. I do lots of things many people may see as weird or fascinating, and sometimes, I get really annoyed because I absolutely hate having to find ways of doing stuff instead of just getting on with it and doing things in the same way everyone else does. I just want to get on and do it without figuring out how I'm going to do it, but sometimes this means that it takes me longer to do certain things.

As I see it, most of the time, finding ways in which I can do stuff is better than me not doing anything at all because I don't want to do things any differently to the way everyone else does. Or perhaps attempting to do a job in the same way as someone like my mum would do it, for example, and then hurting myself because I don't quite have the physical ability to do it the way my mum would do it. For me, my way is better than no way.

But I still wonder how easy it would be to do all those normal day-to-day jobs without having a disability and without having to find new ways of doing them. Sometimes I wonder if people actually think about what they're doing, and how easy it is for them to do things, and what life would be like if they weren't able to do their daily jobs without any struggle. Do people actually think about that? For me, I think about this every day, and I realise that life is a lot harder for me than for most people. But mainly, I think about how lucky I am to be able to do and achieve daily jobs just as everyone else does, because it's better than not being able to do anything at all.

On a certain occasion, when I was around sixteen months old, my family were told by doctors that I would not be able to do anything at all for myself and that I would be wheelchair-bound. You see, sixteen years on, being able to walk and talk and do most things, it's easy for me to say, "Look at me now" and show off about how I proved all the doctors wrong. But I don't really feel like doing that because, even though I can walk and talk and do all the things the doctors said I wouldn't be able to do — and don't get me wrong, I feel blessed that I can do these things — I still have to work twice as hard as everyone else does to be able to live my life. I get exhausted by doing little things, whereas other people don't and could probably do twice as much as I do in a single hour of the day. That might just be down to my laziness sometimes — I'm not sure.

Life's harder for me than it is for most people, so why would I show off and say, "Look at me now" when I was still dealt a tricky card to live with? Just because I proved all the doctors wrong by walking and talking doesn't mean that life's automatically easy for me. Every day is hard, and some days are harder than others. On the other hand, I don't feel sorry for myself because of this, and I don't want to feel sorry for myself at all, because I know I'm very lucky to walk and talk at all. I know there are people out there who can't walk or talk and who aren't as able-bodied as I am.

When I do have bad days and I'm feeling sorry for myself, I sometimes feel a bit guilty about that, because I'm lucky to be able to do even half the things I do in my daily life. I think about what life must be like for those people who have to live their lives confined to a wheelchair, and because of this, I feel I don't have the right to just sit there and feel sorry about how hard my life is.

I also know that, living with a disability, you take things for granted just as able-bodied people do. When I'm doing anything, whether it's something big or small, at any time of day, I don't always think about how fortunate I am to be able to do what I'm doing at that specific moment. And so, yeah, at times I do take life for granted. I think it's a natural thing to do in society. I think we don't realise how lucky we are to be able to live our normal lives every day, and not have to watch other people living their normal lives while all we can do is sit there and dream about normal life, which is what some less fortunate people have to experience.

Living with a disability, it's so irritating to see people treat life as if it were a joke — something we can re-live over and over again — when the truth is, we can't do that. We have a sort of duty to live life as fully as possible; I think, if people started to appreciate life a bit more and all the things that they're fortunate to be able to do in life, it wouldn't be seen as such a joke and more people would see beauty in their daily lives.

Sometimes, I wish there was no such thing as disability at all, so that more people could experience and live a full life, without anything holding them back and stopping them from achieving simple daily things that we all take for granted every day. What a great world that would be, with everyone living the life that they should live and deserve to live, but unfortunately, for some that isn't possible. However, if you are able-bodied and can do whatever you like in life without a struggle, no matter how big or small, please see it as a blessing, as a gift that you have been given by the universe — or whatever you believe in — and appreciate all the things you're able to do in life.

There are loads of people out there who can only dream of being in your shoes and being able to live life without disability and all the restrictions and barriers that come with it. See life as something big, don't take it for granted — you only get to live it once.

Chapter Six

The Frustrations of Being Disabled

*M*essage to Mum from me, speaking aggressively into the text-speaker thing so I don't have to type out the message:

CAN YOU GET ME A TUB OF BEN AND JERRY'S PLEASE, I'LL PAY YOU BACK!

The text message itself comes out nothing like I wanted it to say…

So, I give up on the speaking thing or whatever it's called and just type the text message out with a big sigh.

You see, these are the kinds of things that I have to put up with, being disabled. Being misunderstood, even over the phone, is annoying. When you live with a disability, there are lots of frustrations that come with it. The example that I've mentioned above is just one of the frustrations I face in daily life. As my disability affects my speech and movement, most of my frustrations come from things relating to these two capabilities. Not being understood by people; falling over; people not considering the fact that I'm disabled; these are literally the things that frustrate me, along with other subjects that I'm going to talk about shortly.

As an individual, pretty much all my life I've craved to be like everyone else, be seen to be like everyone else and be treated like everyone else. These three things are what I hope for every day when I wake up. However, now I understand why these three things can't always happen in certain situations, so when there's a good reason why these things can't happen, I understand why not and accept that. Over the years, I've come to accept that I'm different to everyone else and that, sometimes, I need to be treated differently to the way everyone else is treated, and that this is for my benefit. Before I came to accept this, when there were situations where I needed a little bit of help with something — which meant that I wasn't treated as an equal to everyone else around me — I used to get very bitter, to the point where I didn't want any help because it wasn't how everyone else was being treated, even though, at those times, I needed help.

Nowadays, if I need help with something that my disability restricts me from doing but that my friends or family will probably never need help within their lifetimes, I accept the help as I know it will benefit me. But what I don't want to accept and really irritates me is being treated differently for absolutely no reason at all. Even though I'm disabled, I am just like everyone else and firmly believe in equality, not just for myself but for everyone, disabled or not. As a girl with a disability, I haven't really experienced much equality in my seventeen years of being on the planet and this has been very annoying at times, when people have treated me differently to others.

One of the things that frustrates me is being spoken to as though I'm a two-year-old. This happens all the time, in situations where people ought to speak to me in the way they would normally speak to someone of my age, but then they speak to me in a babyish manner. It is not how they would usually speak to a seventeen-year-old girl. When this does happen, I feel like I'm back to being a toddler who's dependent on people. I feel stupid. I feel as though I don't have a single brain cell within my body and that I can't do anything, and that's why the person is speaking to me like that. There aren't many occasions when I feel like I'm ten years younger than I am, but when these situations happen, I feel exactly like that. It's annoying because I don't want people to talk down to me like that: I'm a seventeen-year-old, not a two-year-old, but because I have a disability, I think people's initial reaction can be to treat me as though I'm a child in a nursery and they imagine I'll be all right with it.

I find it so unfair when, for example, I'm with a friend and we're ordering food in a restaurant: the waiter/waitress speaks to my friend as an adult and then turns to take my order and speaks to me like a child. He/she sees that my friend and I are exactly the same age but then sees that I'm physically disabled; they automatically presume they should speak to me like a child because I'm disabled. That's so unfair in my eyes. When that does happen, I feel humiliated because I'm thinking, "Well, do I look stupid? Am I wearing something that makes me look younger than I am?" All these questions I'm asking myself go round and round in my head for the rest of the day.

Sometimes, I feel the need to dress up so that I look like an adult and won't get spoken to like this, but then, on the other hand, I don't want to dress so that I look like my mum and my auntie (for example) rather than dressing as my friends dress themselves. It shouldn't be like that — I shouldn't have to feel the need to do this because some people can't speak to me as they would to others of my age. At other times, I just want to let out the anger I feel at the time, when a person is speaking to me like a child, and I want to scream at them and tell them I don't want to be spoken to like that: I'm not a baby, I'm a seventeen-year-old, so please speak to me like one.

But then I think that'll just make things more awkward than they already are, which would actually make things a whole lot worse. So, most of the time, I just let people speak to me as though I were a child, regardless of how frustrated it makes me feel: I just hide it all. At times, it does upset me, that people just presume how they should treat me because I'm disabled. It sounds crazy, but I feel like I have to write instructions on how I would like to be treated and then give them to everyone I come across during my life. The instructions would be plain and simple. They would simply read:

TREAT AND SPEAK TO ME IN THE SAME WAY YOU WOULD TREAT AND SPEAK TO EVERYONE ELSE.

Even then, I don't think I would be treated as everyone else is treated, even though I should be. I feel as though there will always be someone out there who will see me as different and treat me differently from the way they would treat a non-disabled person, when there isn't a need to do so. This still aggravates me.

Even though most of my frustrations are aimed at the world around me and relate to the way people treat me sometimes, I also get frustrated with myself a lot as well. This might be when I fall over, or when I can't do something, or when I just have days where I simply feel useless because I'm disabled. Sometimes, I have days where I'm hard on myself for not being able to be "normal". These types of frustration mostly occur when I fall over, or when I can't cook a meal for myself like everyone else can, or for some other simple reason that involves my disability.

Most of the time, I'm fine with being disabled and don't really mind being slightly different from everyone else because, from my perspective, I can't change this and so might as well accept it and not dwell on it. But then there are occasions when something happens to me — for example, I fall over in the street because I've lost my balance due to my cerebral palsy. Instantly, all the emotions and anger that I feel towards myself and my disability come to the forefront of my mind: "You're useless, look at you, you've lost your balance, you're so different to everyone else, that's a bad thing". All these thoughts come rushing through my mind. Automatically these thoughts make me see my disability as a negative, as something that I should frown on, that I should be ashamed of. And then I hate myself, just like I used to when I was at primary school.

A fall is like a reminder that I'm different to everyone else, but instead of my just accepting this and understanding that I've just had a fall and it's not the end of the world, I do sometimes see it as the end of the world. At these times, I get so angry with myself for falling over. Why didn't I do this? Why didn't I do that? And so, I just take it out on myself.

Usually, this goes on for only a couple of hours or so, depending how I feel at that time. Alternatively, when I'm feeling a bit down already, and I fall over and that fall comes and hits me in the face with the thought that having a disability is a bad thing, the negative feelings that I experience after this can last for a couple of days. My self-confidence gets knocked because of the fall, with the result that I don't have very much confidence in myself generally.

Sometimes, I also get angry and frustrated with the world and ask questions of the universe (or whatever is out there) such as, "Why me? Why am I the one who had to have a disability? What's wrong with me?". And knowing that these questions may never be answered, it makes me want to give up because what's the point of living as a disabled person when you don't know why or what for? It seems there's no bigger picture to being disabled, you just have to live with it.

But some days I don't want to live with it; some days I just wake up feeling angry that I was given this thing that doesn't make me like everyone else and restricts me from doing what I actually want to do in life. Even though these days happen rarely, they still happen, and they still make me feel like the whole world is against me.

There are so many frustrations I have to live with that come from being disabled. The ones I've spoken about here are only some of the frustrations I have to face. There are so many things I deal with that can at times get me really angry. Sometimes they can go on to impact my mental health, whether it's how the world treats me or that I'm angry with myself for not being able to do things that everyone else can do. They can make me think about whether it's really worth going on and living my life as a disabled person, because I'm sick of dealing with these frustrations on a daily basis, I'm sick of being treat differently, and I'm sick of not being able to do things that everyone else can do.

But of course, it is worth it — everything I do is worth it. Everyone deals with frustrations in their day-to-day lives, but for me, most of my frustrations are directed at my disability. However, I'm willing to face and deal with them in order to get to where I want to be in life. The frustrations represent only a small percentage of what life has to offer and there's a bigger picture beyond focusing on how people treat you or how you feel at times about having a disability. I know there will be times when I'll feel angry, but I also know that these times are completely normal and that I'm allowed to feel like this. I'm only human.

Chapter Seven

Don't Use Those Words

We call one another all kinds of names in our daily lives, don't we, as a way of calling one another to account or joshing the other person about what they've done — whether they've done something stupid or you're trying to be critical. "Oh, you numpty" or "You absolute idiot" — we hear these phrases all the time, as well as other words that are worse than these. I think you get what I mean. But when we're using such words to be spiteful towards one another, we don't really get what these words mean; we don't really think about the context around them or how they can affect people and situations.

Most of the words we use to call people things don't really mean much and are normally just semi-offensive words. But there are some words out there that can be aimed at specific targets and these could be (for example) ethnicity, sexuality, gender, or body type. These are the words I hate the most because I know how it feels when words are aimed at an aspect of a person that they can't really help and that's a part of them. This is because there are words out there that are aimed at people with disabilities.

These words include words such as "retard" or "spastic" and there are others. I hear such words on a daily basis when I'm at college or when I'm shopping. These are the types of word that really get to me and make me very angry, because these words shouldn't exist, they shouldn't be out there so that people can label having a disability as some sort of bad thing, something people should be ashamed of. I often hear these kinds of word spoken by people who are my age. It makes it even harder because I feel as though even my generation hasn't come to accept disability as a completely normal thing, in the same way they might accept other things. I hear comments like, "Oh, you're such a spastic", and every time I hear comments like this, I just want to turn round to that person and ask them questions like, "Do you actually know the meaning behind that word?" or "What makes you think using words that are really offensive for people with disabilities is OK?".

Sometimes, I feel as though people do think it's not OK to use certain words that might be offensive to some people, yet when words such as "spastic" are used, it seems it's OK — it's fine, you can use that word, it won't offend anyone. But it does offend; it offends me. For me, the words "spastic" and "retard" really hit home and make me feel a whole range of emotions, anger, sadness, and confusion. Every time I hear these words, the first thought that comes into my mind is that I'm not fully accepted into society, that I'm frowned upon for being disabled. Therefore, I'm not considered to be someone who is "good" or "accepted" in society, just because I have a disability.

It's as though, for people out there, my feelings are forgotten about as someone who is living with a disability, and that my feelings are not taken into account by society. I feel as though people think it's normal to label a disability as a bad thing by using horrible, offensive words to describe it. To them, they are probably just words they use to try and be mean towards someone, implying that the object of their comment is somehow bad. But to me, it's implying that I should be ashamed of my disability because society is still labelling it as something to be embarrassed about. It doesn't matter when or where I hear it, or who I've heard it from, whenever I hear words like this, it's like a smack in the face.

It's as though I don't matter to the world at all, and I'm not considered to be a human who has feelings and gets hurt by things that are said. I feel as though I'm living with some sort of disease, a disease that no one wants and everyone hates. As people hate it so much, they turn it into some sort of joke and use the name of this disease as something offensive and to feel bad about. I think we all hate being called names; often, the names we are called or that we use to call others are something unpleasant or rude.

I never really understood what the words "spastic" or "retard" meant, and then I started hearing people calling others by these names and kept hearing them from time to time. As with any other swear words that I've ever heard, I started to wonder why people called others by these words and what they meant. At first, I thought they meant something else that was bad or rude and you would be seen as cool for saying them in the school playground, where everyone would hear you say those words and laugh, because that's what kids do, especially at primary school. So I was intrigued to discover the meaning behind the words, so that I would then know what it meant if someone called you or someone else by those words. I never thought they were about disabilities.

But when I did find out the real meaning behind these words, I was so confused. I was told that they did refer to being disabled, that the term "spastic" or the term "retard" was a harsh way of describing someone with a disability. You should bear in mind that I was just ten years old at the time and was still trying to figure out why I was disabled and different to everyone else — obviously I didn't like that very much. So to learn that there were swear words out there which were negative (in my eyes, at least) about disabilities confused me even more. I just couldn't understand why there would be such words that described people with disabilities in a very cruel way.

Was it bad that I was disabled? Do people really hate disabled people so much that they thought they'd come up with horrible names to describe them? Was it bad that I wasn't like everyone else and didn't walk or talk like everyone else? All these questions were going round and round in my head. At the time, I was being bullied at school as well, so I put the reason I was being bullied down to being disabled and that it was so hard for people to accept. That just made me hate being disabled even more than I already did.

But deep down, I knew that having a disability wasn't the problem at all, it was how people saw it that was the problem. For some time, I've been desperate for people to be less negative about the concept of being disabled and to understand that there is no shame in having a disability. But then, I hear words like the ones I've mentioned above, and it's as though things will never change, there's always going to be this negative view about how disabilities are seen in the world — whether it's today, next month, or a few years from now.

That's what really gets to me, because I expect to live a life that isn't typical of a normal life due to my disability. I don't expect to live fully independently, I don't expect to meet the man of my dreams and get married, I don't expect to have children with that man. To me, these are dreams that I don't think will ever come true. Maybe I can live independently — I only need myself in order to do that, and maybe I'll need a bit of help from family and friends, but as for the other aspirations, in my eyes, it will be a miracle if they ever happen.

All of this is down to people's negative attitudes towards disabled people, and the fact that disability is not seen as 'normal' in society. These are harsh ways to describe someone as, let's face it, no one wants to be disabled and different from everyone else. I sometimes think that, if those words didn't exist at all, then maybe disabled people like me might have been or might now be accepted into society a lot more readily than they are, because disability wouldn't be seen as such a taboo subject, and everyone would just see us as normal people in society.

However, because these words exist, what I've hoped for isn't the case. Whenever I hear the word "spastic", I see that someone is calling someone else "disabled" as an insult that's being made in order to offend that person. But that is utterly wrong in my view. Calling a person disabled in order to insult and offend them is an insult to me and all the other people around the world living with disabilities. I find it very offensive that, in a way, my condition is being used as an insult. How does that make me look to the world? There's no wonder why I've been seen as different and in a negative light all my life, because I'm living with something that is seen by the world as negative.

It shouldn't be like this: disabilities aren't bad at all, so shame on you if you are one of the people who do see them as bad and feel the need to use them to insult another person. I am not bad, and neither is my disability. Actually, I quite like the fact that I'm disabled and don't find it negative at all; sure, it's hard at times, but it doesn't mean people should use it as an insult. What's so bad about having a disability? We're still people, there's no need to make a harsh joke out of it and try to get people down by calling them disabled — it's really not that funny.

Maybe if we started teaching people about disabilities, so that it's just seen as a normal part of daily life, then perhaps this situation will change? Every time you call someone a "retard" or a "spastic" because they're being stupid or silly, actually think about what you're saying, what you're implying, because you never know who might hear those words. At that very moment, a disabled person could be right next to you when you're uttering such words and you never know what the effect of those words could be on someone who has a disability.

I hate the fact that my condition is used as an insult and a little pain stabs inside me whenever I hear these insulting words. I've asked many people, many times not to use words like these in order to insult someone and I really hope they realise what the words actually mean and who they might offend and affect when they use them in order to be offensive. I think we should start seeing having a disability in a positive light; we shouldn't see it as such a bad thing and should stop using disability as an insult, because it shouldn't be an insult at all. Let's start teaching people this so that hopefully, one day, words like "spastic" and "retard" will no longer exist.

I am not an insult. I am a person with feelings, just like you.

Chapter Eight

The Acceptance of Being Different

Acceptance is a big thing for me and it's a big part of my life as well. As someone who hasn't been accepted by others at times, and hasn't really accepted themselves at times either, I crave it very much. You see, in a world where there's a lot of judgements made by people towards other people for many different reasons — for instance, how that person looks, what they wear, or even who they are as an individual, I feel that acceptance isn't really such a big thing and it should be something we can all do. Of course, we all have a tendency to judge people, but people often don't realise what judgement can do to someone — how it can make them feel. I know exactly what it feels like to be judged for who you are and not being able to do anything about it.

As I've just said, my disability has meant that, at times, I haven't been accepted by others or even accepted myself. Because I'm disabled, I think that people may see this as something that's entirely different to them. This automatically leads them to judge me, as that's probably their first reaction when they meet me for the very first time. As I've said elsewhere, people don't like "different", everyone wants to be the same, and so when they see that I'm different, they don't like that. They tend to have negative emotions towards me which they might not have when first meeting non-disabled people. Non-disabled people are not as alien to them as I may seem.

This has led to my disability not being accepted by others on many different occasions. What I've realised over the years is that it's usually people of my own age who don't really accept me, because my generation is still quite young and so they don't fully understand disabilities and the differences there are, as the older generation might. In school, this was a big issue — mainly in primary school but also sometimes in secondary school. As a young girl, I just wanted to be accepted by everyone else and to be seen like everyone else was. As shallow as it sounds, I wanted to be seen as cool, but I was seen as the complete opposite. I remember, in the early years at primary school, being stared at a lot. But these weren't the type of stares you might get when everyone is fascinated by you; they were the type of stares you get when people find you weird and want to stay away from you.

At first, I didn't really notice as I was so young and all that was on my mind was playing with toys and what fairy princess dress I was going to put on that day. But when I eventually noticed the evil stares I was getting from other children, I was very confused. Had I done something wrong? Was there something on my face? What was it? Why was I being stared at? I didn't really take any notice of it at first, as we were kids and did stare at people and things; it was in our nature to do so. If I was introduced to a new person, my first reaction would be to stare at them. That's what kids do. But then I realised that I wasn't a new person, I had been in the same class as some of the other kids for a few years by then, and all the other kids never stared at one another — it was just me that was getting the weird looks.

I started to wonder why that was, and as it continued, I also started to get mean comments made about my disability. Then I figured out why I was treated differently from all the other kids. The realisation that I wasn't accepted because I was disabled made me feel really sad as, before then, I didn't really realise how much of a big issue being disabled was for all the other children. Before then, I didn't really take much notice of my disability, I knew I had it, but it wasn't such an issue for me. When I became aware that it was an issue for everyone else, it then became an issue for me.

If young children don't grow up with a disabled person in their lives, disability is hard for them to understand and accept because, from their perspective, it's so peculiar and they don't like the thought of anything peculiar. In society in general, I don't think children are really taught about disabilities unless they have an association with someone who is disabled. Because of this, if they were to come across someone with a disability, they wouldn't know what to do, as they wouldn't understand why that individual is different to them and to everyone else. For me, this is what led to me not being accepted by my peers, because they didn't have a full understanding of why I was different. It was really irritating as I wanted to be treated like everyone else and yet I wasn't.

I saw everyone else making friends, but I was kind of on the sidelines, watching everyone else interact with one another and play with one another. I was just there, watching all this happen and wishing that I could experience making friends and be a normal schoolchild one day. But that never happened in the early years of primary school, because I was different and therefore I wasn't accepted.

Looking back now and understanding the absence of knowledge children have, I can see why my classmates found it quite hard to accept me. However, at the age of seventeen, what I don't understand is why I'm still not accepted by others of my age or near my age. Perhaps it's just me, but surely, at the age of seventeen, you will have heard about disabilities, and you'll understand that not everyone is the same and that some people are different? So why is this still so hard for people of my age to accept? Why is it so hard for people to treat me like a normal person?

To this day, I just don't get why, from time to time, I feel as though I'm not accepted in society or amongst others of my generation, when surely people have better knowledge of disabilities these days. When these situations occur, I get quite angry and upset, as I've put up with not being accepted for so long — especially by my generation. I'm so fed up with people not giving me the time of day or not getting to know me, because of the simple fact that I'm disabled. This may be a presumption on my behalf, but if I were to sit at a table with two people who are friends and then these friends take notice of another person without a disability, who may also be sitting at the table and who has only just met them — as I have, to me it's quite obvious that people won't want to give me the time of day in such a situation, because I'm different.

I can see that it's hard for people to come to terms with disability and people do tell me to be patient with others and let them get used to me and my disability. But the point is that I've been being patient all my life, waiting for people to accept me. Sometimes, I've waited for weeks or even months for this to happen and now I'm fed up with being patient with people all the time, so that they can 'get used to me'. I'm just like everyone else so why can't people understand that?

It would be great if, one day, I could just walk into a room full of people who are complete strangers of my own age and actually make friends with new people straightaway, like everyone else does. I've always wanted this to happen, but the truth is, it never has. When I walk into a room where there are new people of my age whom I haven't met before, I feel somehow left out, because I sense that people aren't giving me the time of day. I remember feeling like this in my first year of college and just wanting to feel accepted by people on my course, but I sensed people didn't fully accept me. It's hard when people don't accept you; the thought and the reality of not being accepted make you not want to accept yourself.

There have been times when, personally, I didn't want to accept the fact that I had a disability. I hated the fact that I didn't sound like everyone else when I talked, or didn't walk like everyone else, or couldn't do all the things that everyone else could do. I just didn't want to accept that I was different from everyone else. I guess, for a while, I saw myself as useless and less of a person because I was disabled. You could say that, for a while, I tried fixing myself. I tried hiding my disability from the world because I was so embarrassed about it.

I would try my very hardest to walk like everyone else did, without a limp, and every time I tried that, my muscles would ache from the strain of trying my hardest to walk normally, because that wasn't my natural way of walking and it didn't benefit me or my body at all.

But I didn't care about how my muscles felt from the strain of trying to walk like everyone else: all that mattered to me was that I didn't look disabled to everyone else.

After years of not wanting to accept my disability or accept myself for who I was, hating every single part of myself because I thought I was worthless for being disabled, I experienced the strain of being emotionally exhausted from hating myself. Trying to hide my disability didn't do me any favours at all, it just made me feel sad all the time, because I wasn't happy with myself in any shape or form. I didn't feel good about myself at all, I hated being disabled and just didn't see the point of life any more. I didn't want to live life in my own body because I thought that I wouldn't be able to live a life at all. Then, one day, someone said something to me.

They said something along these lines: you shouldn't hide your disability because, if you do that, you are pretty much hiding yourself away from the world and everything else; accepting yourself is the first step towards loving yourself and fully loving life. Those words stuck with me for a long time, and I guess I realised that, from that point, I could see I wasn't living a happy life at all because I hated myself, which made me hate life itself.

I was so obsessed with trying to hide my disability that I wasn't actually living. I was existing. Looking back, it saddens me to know how much I really did despise myself and how much I despised my disability, when in fact my disability was a part of what made me a person, but I didn't see that. I think that, if I had been more accepted by my peers and if my disability hadn't been seen as a bad thing, then maybe I wouldn't have hated myself as I did and would have been able to accept my disability a lot more than I did.

If children were taught about disabilities from a young age, I think disabled people would feel more accepted in the world, because disability would be a normal part of society and fewer disabled people would see their disability as a bad thing and would feel more confident about being disabled. Being disabled isn't a bad thing, as I used to think it was, and I think that, if acceptance of disabilities became more prevalent, then, over time, more and more people would see that. So, if you do have a disability, please see the bigger picture and accept it, because it's one of the best parts of you, for so many reasons. So please learn to accept your disability, but most importantly, accept yourself.

Chapter Nine

Not a Typical Teenage Girl

My disability obviously means that I'm different to most girls of my age. I don't do things that other teenage girls do. I don't go to parties, I don't hang out in a field at night drinking, I don't do all the normal stuff that teenagers do. My life is the complete opposite of a non-disabled teenager's life. However, it hasn't stopped me from wondering what life is like for other teenage girls and what they must get up to, or whether they have fun or not. Of course they do — what teenager doesn't have fun partying, getting drunk, and snogging people at random?

You see, my teens have been somewhat different. Well, for one, I haven't snogged a boy and don't really plan on doing so anytime soon. My teenagehood has meant that I've missed out on a lot of things teenagers do every day. Whether it's because I've struggled with making friends or I've had to go to a doctor's appointment instead of going on a girlie day out, I haven't had the full experience of being a normal teenage girl, as most girls of my age would do.

Unfortunately, even though I've missed out on a lot in my teens, what I haven't missed out on are the joys of puberty. Oh yes, I may be disabled, but puberty is something I have most certainly experienced. I'm still a teen and every teen goes through it. How typical is that? I got to experience the worst parts of being a teen (which is puberty and being hormonal) but have never properly been able to experience all the fun parts, as everyone else of my age has. To be honest with you, if I could trade the experience of going through puberty and all the bad bits about being a teen in order to experience the social side of it, I would: I've always wanted to be a social butterfly (or whatever term you prefer), just like others of my age.

I've always wanted to get drunk in a park somewhere with my friends and go to house parties all the time, but the social aspect of being disabled has meant that, for me, it hasn't been like this most of the time. In a way, I feel as though I've been robbed of experiencing the full monty of teenagehood. I believe this is definitely down to the social side of it, because I've never really struggled with growing up and going through body changes; what I have struggled with is making friends. I've always struggled with making friends. As I've stated previously: I'm different and nobody likes "different", especially in my age group. So, because of this, I haven't been invited out into a field to get drunk and have the best night ever.

Ed Sheeran once wrote a song called "Castle on the Hill". It's basically about his teens and how good those years were, spent with him going out with his friends, smoking and getting drunk every night and just simply doing the normal teenage things that teenagers do. Every time I listen to that song and the lyrics, I listen to each word he sings, and think to myself, "Where was all of this for me, why didn't I do all that stuff Ed did when he was a teenager?". Every time I listen to that song, taking each word of the lyrics in, a realisation hits me that I've been robbed, in a way, of being a normal teenager.

Sometimes, it makes me wonder what my teens would have been like if I hadn't been disabled. Would I have got into smoking and drinking in a dark field with a bunch of people on school nights? Or got my first ever snog at a house party aged sixteen after being sick all over the floor from being way too drunk? For the adults reading this, you'll probably be thinking, "Well, why do you wish you had done all of that, none of it's any fun?". But to most teenagers it is fun, and as I'm coming to the end of my teens, I'm realising that I've missed out on a lot of that fun.

I remember going through my early teens, watching people go out and get drunk at the age of thirteen, because that's the kind of thing people of my generation did at that age. I remember thinking about doing all the stuff that teens do at that age as well, while I was just left wishing I could be going out and getting drunk, like everyone else. But the thing is, I was never invited to those kinds of events, and I think people just presumed I wouldn't be able to do all the things they could do, because of my disability. Because of this, for a long time, I was just sitting on the sidelines while everyone else went out and had fun.

The hardest thing for me was hearing about a party that my friendship group at the time were planning. I would hear all about it at school — where it was, who was going, what day it was on, who was going with whom, who was wearing what. These are the kinds of things I would hear while my friendship group were having a full-on conversation about the party that was happening without me — even though I was, or I thought I was, a member of the friendship group and their friend at the time. And then, after hearing about it all week at school, when the party was taking place that weekend, I would see my friends' stories on Snapchat (where people would place pictures and videos of what they were doing), and all the photos and videos of the party, what they were doing at the party and how much fun they were having, all over social media.

For me, this was absolute crap. I felt so left out, not part of anything at all, and very different to my peers at school. For a while, I wasn't invited to anything and was always being left out. And then, when I was sixteen and in a different friendship group, I finally got invited to my first-ever house party. At this point, everyone else of my age had already been to a house party, but this was a new thing to me, and I couldn't believe that I was actually going to one. I didn't know what to wear or whether the person who was hosting the party needed me to bring anything. I knew nothing about what to do. It was like a dream for me, and as dramatic as it sounds, it just didn't seem real at all. Then the night of the party came, and I was walking up to the front door of the house where the party was taking place and being welcomed in and then stepping into the party itself, with loud music blaring and people standing there with drinks in their hands chatting (or, in the case of the drunker ones, dancing in the corner). For that one night, you could say, I actually experienced part of what it was like to be a normal teenager for the very first time.

Now, if you're a teenager — or even if you're an adult — reading this, having experienced this yourself when you were a teenager, you're probably wondering why going to a house party was a big deal for me, because it probably was or is the norm for you to go to house parties every now and then. But when you've missed out on doing things you haven't done but everyone else has, it's kind of a big deal; you never would've thought you'd be attending a house party when you've missed out on going to house parties for so long in your teens — because you're different. It's kind of surreal.

I think the only time that I felt like a normal teenager was when I was fifteen or sixteen; I started to get invited to house parties and everything, but that was it. That was the only time I got invited as, after that, I'd left school, so I didn't see people from school who might have invited me to these house parties again. I had to make new friends, which was much harder for me to do at college. There was only a year and a half in my teens when I felt like a normal teen. That was it. For the rest of my teens, I felt different from most other teens.

Apart from that year and a half, living with siblings around my age who were also teens was hard, as I would see them do normal teenage things, such as going out with their friends and going to parties whilst I was stuck at home, doing none of that, feeling left out. I was a bit jealous of my siblings — no, really jealous of them in fact — to the point where I just wanted to cry every time they went out to parties and stuff, about how unfair it was that they were going out and doing stuff and I wasn't.

I didn't like the fact that they got to experience all the normal things that I wanted to experience as a teen, while I was just sitting at home doing the exact opposite. I desperately wanted to be like them and do all the stuff they did, but I didn't get the opportunity to do so. I actually liked the times when they weren't being invited out to places by their friends, because it made me feel less left out and more as though I was "normal". But most of the time they were invited out, which meant that, most of the time, I did feel left out and didn't feel "normal".

Doctor's appointments were another barrier, stopping me from being a teenager. Even though I wasn't going out as much as others did, on the very rare occasions when I was invited out by friends, sometimes I couldn't go because I had a previously arranged doctor's appointment I had to attend about my disability. An example would be an invitation to go on a shopping trip with my friends, it would be so irritating to say no to this, because I had to go to a doctor's appointment instead.

I didn't have a choice between whether to go out shopping with my mates or to go to the doctor's appointment; no matter what, the doctor's appointment would always win. So I missed out on a day out with my friends, which was quite a rare event. Doctor's appointments getting in the way of my social life was yet another experience I had to endure as a teen. It was so annoying. But on a more positive note, I haven't really had that many doctor's appointments in my teens. But it's no less frustrating when an appointment crops up and gets in the way of my social life.

I guess this is another thing that differentiates me from most other people — having to go to more doctor's appointments than people generally have to attend, because I've got a disability and they want to see how I'm managing with it. I used to hate these doctor's appointments when I was in my early teens as, yet again, I felt like an outsider who was missing out on a lot. Even when I was taken out of school for an appointment (most kids would love as it would mean they'd miss a couple of hours of school), I hated it. I hated missing out on school to have to go and see a specialist or a doctor about my disability because I wasn't attending school and learning like all my peers were. I simply didn't want to go and see a specialist about how I was getting on with my mobility and whether I had any issues relating to it.

As boring as it sounds, I wanted to be learning stuff from a textbook like everyone else. Well, not in maths or science because I hated those two subjects and when I had those lessons, I wouldn't mind missing them to go to a doctor's appointment. But most of the time, when I did have to miss school to attend an appointment, I felt I'd rather be at school with all my friends. I simply hated doctor's appointments, that was it.

I think being a disabled teen has had its positives and its negatives. I sometimes think that, if I weren't disabled, I would have taken life a lot more for granted than I do. Maybe I would have wasted my life by going down the route of drugs and alcohol like some teens do, or maybe not, I don't know. I think having a disability makes me see the importance of life and what it has to offer, and even though I've missed out on going to parties and other social activities, I've had amazing opportunities which I probably wouldn't have had if I weren't disabled. I think being disabled has set me on a great path in life so, because of that, I don't mind being different from other teens. I've got a lot ahead of me, and call me stupid, but I have a feeling that's down to my disability and how it makes me view life. What I'm saying is that I would happily miss out on all the things most teens do to get to where I am today because, in my eyes, where I am today is way better than partying.

Chapter Ten

My Bullying Story

O ne thing the doctors don't tell you and your family about when you first get diagnosed, is how other kids your age or even adults, can be so misunderstanding towards you or your needs. This was possibly one of the most difficult things for me growing up with cerebral palsy was that other kids in my year at school couldn't accept me for who I was and couldn't stand having a friend that was a little different to them. This sometimes resulted in bullying.

To this day, what happened to me with regards to my bullying still has an impact on me and there are still times where I get affected by it and I am still having to process it as to be completely honest, there are some bits that I don't fully understand myself. I am going to be completely honest with you guys and share with you what happened during my time at primary school and sometimes in secondary school as well, not to make you feel sorry for me, but to reach out to those who have been bullied and who are being bullied, to make them feel like they're not alone.

I guess you could say being disabled, you expect to be called names due to your disability due to the attitudes that are behind it that have stemmed from the generations before us. However, being bullied is something that no one should go through whether they're disabled or not. I didn't believe that was the case for me until now, many years later when I've come back to process it.

For me, my actual bullying story started when I was about eight-years-old. Before then, I wasn't really bullied, however, at the same time, I wasn't really accepted as well. I think because I was vulnerable, my bullies saw that as an easy target and thrived off that and then proceeded to then go onto bully me. I remember it started off with evil glares from some of the girls in my year and I didn't really know what for either. Had I done something wrong? I didn't think so. I was just a girl who was going about my normal school day, and so this confused me quite a bit as I didn't know what was going on and what I had supposedly done wrong and so it did make me feel a bit uncomfortable but it didn't really affect me that much.

However, that soon escalated. The evil stares turned into evil comments. About the way I ate, about the way I looked, about the way I walked and talked, and about other things as well. Now the confusing thing about this is that the bullies weren't just kids that I didn't even know and rarely spoke to before all of this started happening, they were the group of girls that I wanted to be friends with, the group of girls I wanted to play with at lunchtime, the group of girls who were friendly to me at times during these periods, but who would become nasty and ditch me at other times as well and then went onto give me nasty comments about everything about me. They were the group of girls who I was trying to seek their full approval from but never got it.

The first few incidents that happened was when some of the girls in the group said that I couldn't sit with them at break times and refused me a space at the table that they were sitting at. I remember going over there with my lunch box and waiting for them to offer me a space at the table. Instead, they started to smirk at each other as if something weird had approached them and started whispering to one another and giggling which made me feel uncomfortable. What happened then was one of the girls turned around to me and said that none of them wanted me to sit with them. You would think that by this point, I would have gone 'suit yourselves' and left them to it to go and find another group of friends who would accept me for who I was and value me as a person. Instead I started pleading with some of these girls to let me sit with them and begged them to offer me that seat. Eventually, the teacher intervened and told them to let me sit with them in which they did as they didn't really have a choice. But during that lunchtime, they would make comments to one another, give me glares and even criticise me on what I was doing. I couldn't do anything right for them.

This made me feel absolutely rubbish. All I wanted to do was to have friends and fit in with everyone else, who doesn't, but this didn't happen. Every lunchtime was like this. I would go over there and get eyes rolled at me or comments made to me if I did or said something that they didn't like, but I accepted it. I thought I deserved all of that due to being disabled. Looking back now as I'm writing this, I should've walked away and left the group to go and find new friends who actually appreciated me, but the thing was as shallow as it sounds they were the cool girls of the year and as a little girl who didn't like herself very much and couldn't understand why I was different, I wanted to be seen as cool so that my disability could be hidden in a way and so I thought the only way to do this was to hang around with them in order to be one of the cool girls and be accepted by everyone. But by doing this, it only got worse.

An incident that happened with two of the girls that to this day still stands out to me, was me and those two girls were in the cloakroom one time. I was probably trying to speak to them and so that's why I stayed behind with those two girls whilst the rest of the class was in the classroom after just coming in after break, to try and be friends with them. Anyway, all of a sudden one of the girls picked up one of my school shoes that I was about to put on and threw it to the floor and began kicking it around everywhere and shouting something but I can't remember what.

What I should've done is picked up my shoe and told her to stop, but I was weak and I believed everything that they had commented on about me up to that day, that I was disgusting and weird and many other things as well, and I didn't have the guts to do that. Instead, what I did was I joined in and started kicking the shoe around as well but inside I was breaking. Why was my 'friend' kicking my stuff around and disrespecting me? What had I done? I just wanted their approval, hence why I joined in on kicking my own property around, because I didn't want them to hate me even more than they already had seemed to have done. But after that incident, I felt crushed, like my heart had been ripped out of my chest and stamped on. I never told anyone about that incident, and when the teacher saw me crying after it had happened, I just made up a story.

There were other incidents that would occur regularly. For instance, every time that I went to play with some of the girls, they would laugh at me and start running away from me. As I wanted to play with them, I would chase after them to catch up and so it would turn into a chase game where every time I caught up with them, they would laugh at me and start running away. It would sometimes happen within the classroom as well and I even got a pen thrown at me one time. The comments about what I did never stopped, I would always get criticised and glared at. At playtime when they wanted to play football, they would pick two team leaders and then the team leaders would chose who they wanted in their team and I was always the last one to be picked, but even that would result in an argument between the two teams right in front of me because neither of them wanted me on their team, and then when the game had started and I couldn't kick the ball right, for example, due to my disability, I would be ganged up on and pretty much told how useless I was for not being able to do one simple thing.

They loved calling me names. 'Goofy' and 'disgusting' were the most common terms that they called me, and even though it wasn't to my face, I always knew that they were saying stuff about me as they would always play Chinese whispers around the table that we all sat at for lunch and leave me out so that I couldn't join in. I did confront them about this and loads of other stuff as well but it would always be turned around on me and I was made to be the issue, not them. I even had to apologise to one of them because apparently, I upset her because I had cried over something that she and her friend had done to upset me. One time when I was crying over what they did, they said that I sounded like a woman giving birth and that I was a cow. How? I was only reacting to what they had done to me. How was it my fault?

In secondary school, it didn't really happen as much, but as I was trying to still be friends with them and as I was still trying to get their approval, there were times where they would still gang up on me and I would get blamed for stuff that I hadn't done and put down a lot by them because of my appearance and some other kids would call me names such as 'spastic' and 'retard'; one of them even poured a drink over me once in a group argument where I wasn't doing anything apart from just standing there, which confused me a bit because why was the drink poured over me when I wasn't the one that they were arguing with. But luckily those times didn't have as much of an impact as it had done in primary school as I had friends to support me, but it still hurt, just not as much.

You see, the confusing thing about all of this is that they weren't nasty all of the time and there were times where they were nice to me, and I think because of those times, and that they never laid a hand on me in all of this, it has taken me a while to accept that I was bullied and I think I protected them a bit as well because I tried to hide what was happening away from everyone. But just because I wasn't punched or kicked or beaten up, doesn't mean that I wasn't bullied. But as I'm writing this, I am refusing to let this bring me down any more. I don't want any sympathy for sharing this with you guys, that isn't why I shared it. I am sharing this because I want to help people out there who have been through similar situations to what I have been through, to feel as if they're not alone. I think as a society, we need to start educating future generations on the differences that are out there in the world so that situations like this are less likely to happen. It saddens me that if I wasn't bullied, I probably would've accepted my disability a lot more sooner than what I had done, and I don't want anyone going through that and what I went through. I hope that by me sharing my story, I can at least help one person who may be going through this feel less alone. I also hope for a kinder world where we are all accepted as we are and everyone can be kind to one another. So, please be kind to one another, you never know, it can make someone's day.

Chapter Eleven

A Little Bit Behind

One day, I was watching my older sister do her makeup in the mirror as she was getting ready for school — doing her eyebrows, then her eyeliner, then her foundation and so on. I used to watch her doing her makeup every morning. Not in a creepy way, spying on her from round the corner or staring right at her with my eyes wide open. I think eventually she would have told me to f… off if I had done that. Normally we would be having a conversation about something, and whilst we talked, I used to watch how she did her make up. It always fascinated me. The steadiness of her hand as she applied her eyeliner and mascara or how she didn't poke herself in the eye with an eye makeup brush. I would just sit there, wondering how she did it.

To me, my sister doing her makeup was something that her year group did. I was way too young to be applying makeup and so it didn't bother me that I couldn't put makeup on, as no one my age had got into doing that yet. But when all the girls of my age started wearing makeup, it panicked me a bit because I couldn't do makeup at all. So, as I was at the age when I really wanted to wear makeup, I started practising. Let's put it this way, my first-ever attempt at applying my own makeup was quite something, to say the least! I started wearing makeup at the same time as some of my friends at school, and while they learnt how to put on makeup within a couple of months and started wearing it out and about, it took me years to put makeup on myself before I could even consider wearing it out and about. I was a little bit behind them, you might say, with that aspect of girlhood (or whatever term you care to use to describe growing up).

But doing my own makeup isn't the only aspect of my life where I've been a little bit behind other girls of my age. All my life I've been behind everyone else of my age with doing various things. You could call it a race, in which everyone else of my age is in front and I'm right at the back, trying to catch up with them. All my life I've been trying to catch up with everyone else in doing certain physical tasks. This is understandable as I've always had a physical disability that limits me from doing some things, and so I'm going to be doing these things a bit later in life than other people.

I guess my family and I knew that, from the day when I actually got diagnosed with cerebral palsy, this was always going to create difficulties for me throughout my life. From the day I was born, I was already at the back of the race, trying to catch up with all the other babies. It was really noticeable that my twin brother and I were very different from each other, and I don't mean this in the context where one of us cries all the time while the other one doesn't — although this is true, and I was such a brat as a baby — as every baby is different. I'm saying this in the context that my mobility and development were completely different from the way my brother developed. My development was actually different to most babies' development, not just my brother's. I didn't lift my legs up in the air like most babies would; I didn't sit up at six months old like most babies would; I just wasn't like most babies. Although I did cry, I cried a lot, which is what made me a "bratty" baby.

My development wasn't the same as most babies' is. Instead, during my first year, I was quite rigid: I couldn't sit up, I couldn't crawl, the only thing I could do was roll over. Most babies can do all these things and a lot more. With the benefit of hindsight, this was obviously a sign that I had cerebral palsy, which was subsequently diagnosed when I was just over one year old. This explained why my development was completely different to my twin brother's. My development as a baby illustrated the first time that I was behind on different stages of life, but it wouldn't be the last.

As a kid, the various stages of my development showed how behind I was. I didn't walk at the age of one like everyone else did at that age. Instead, I took my first steps at the age of three or four, I said my first-ever word aged four — so it was quite obvious from an early age that I was behind with the normal activities in life. I was at the back of the race, behind everyone else.

Throughout my childhood, cerebral palsy restricted me from doing all the things other children were doing, and I think that's part of the reason why I struggled with making friends and interacting with other children, because I couldn't do what they could do. I would watch all my friends in class do simple things like using scissors to cut something out, and because I couldn't use scissors due to difficulties with my motor skills, that little thing I couldn't do created a big barrier, preventing me from interacting with others — all because I couldn't use scissors and therefore couldn't join in on activities with other children.

Being behind physically has always upset me at various points in different ways. Seeing people of your age doing stuff that you can't do is hard, because you want to be able to do the stuff they are doing, to feel a part of something, but you physically can't do it. I remember, when I was younger and in primary school, my peers and I used to go to swimming classes every Tuesday and on one occasion there was a swimming competition. As I couldn't swim but all my peers could, I wasn't able to join in the swimming competition, and so I had to sit and watch the competition take place and see all the other children compete in it.

Now, I absolutely love swimming — I always have, I love being in water as I feel light in it, which is something I don't feel when I'm out of the water. Seeing all your peers doing something that you love but can't do makes you feel kind of left out and that you're not part of anything at all. I was so angry that I had this disability which was stopping me from doing what I loved. I really wanted to join in, but I couldn't because I couldn't swim, yet all the other children could.

But I was really determined to change all that. I was determined to swim. So when I was around fifteen years old, I took part in one-to-one swimming lessons, and learnt how to swim. Yeah, I was fifteen years old and not five years old, which is when everyone else probably learnt to swim, and so I was very behind with being able to swim. But this didn't bother me, all that mattered was that I should achieve my dream of being able to swim, even though I achieved it a bit later in life than everyone else.

I think being behind everyone else from a physical point of view was already upsetting to me as a child because I couldn't join in with certain activities, but it then became even more upsetting and a massive problem when I became a teenager. Every other girl was getting into makeup and hair, just as my sister was by this point, and I couldn't get into it properly, like all the other girls did, because physically I couldn't do my hair and makeup as they did. I think the pressure of wanting to be like everyone else made it even worse, but mainly, there was the sense that you weren't being your age and weren't normal because you couldn't do what your friends were doing. That really got to me.

In a way, I felt abnormal as a person just because I couldn't do my hair and makeup. Every time I tried, I failed and turned out looking awful. I would have a full-on meltdown in my bathroom, because I couldn't put on eyeliner and then I'd be in a bad mood and the rest of the day would be a write-off. I was very interested in getting into makeup so that I could be like everyone else, but I couldn't do it. When I failed at doing something for the first time, whether applying makeup or anything else, it would be the end of the world and I just wanted to give up on life.

It got to the point where my family and my best friend had to step in, because it upset me so much that I couldn't apply makeup or do other stuff that girls of my age were doing. And so my best friend, who had already got into makeup like everyone else, sat me down and got a load of my makeup out, and we spent hours at my dressing table as she taught me how to put on makeup. There were many times when I would get frustrated with myself for not being able to do something and she would calm me down and tell me that it's all down to practice. She said that the more I practised, the better I would get at doing it. I think it was her advice which made me realise that, if I kept practising doing my makeup, then I *would* eventually be able to do it. And so that's what I did — I practised doing my makeup and eventually got there, so that now I can do my makeup like everyone else.

I think everything we learn to do in our lives takes practice, we can't just do something straight away, at our first attempt. What I've come to realise is that, no matter who we are, we're always behind someone else when trying to do something, or else we're not behind at all, but do different things at our own pace. Nowadays, if I can't do something and everyone else can, that's OK, I will get there at my own pace, no matter how long it takes me to achieve it.

We shouldn't really be concerned if someone can't do something, because not everyone can do what others can. I wish I had seen the real meaning of this earlier in life, as I wouldn't have put so much pressure on myself to be like everyone else. We're all different, disabled or not, and some of us can do things that others may not be able to do at that point in their lives, or may never be able to do. If we're behind with some things that others can do, that's OK, we will get there.

Chapter Twelve

Making Adjustments

A big part of living with cerebral palsy is making continual adjustments on a daily basis. I can't do stuff in the same way that other people can do things. I can't lift a pan of boiling hot water and then carry it over to the sink with one hand; things like this are just impossible for me to do because I'm restricted by my disability. If I were even to attempt lifting a bowl of boiling hot water and carrying it to the sink using just one hand, I would end up burning myself quite badly. However, just because I can't do normal daily things in the same way that everyone else does them, doesn't mean that I wouldn't be able to do them at all.

This is where the adjustments come in. I've always wanted to be independent, not having to rely so much on people doing everything for me. In order for me to have some sort of independence — which is what I want — I have to adjust how I do certain things so that I can do them in some form, and so that I don't put myself at risk of self-harm. I've always been determined to do things myself and so, when I can't do them in the way my mum does them, it's frustrating. But finding adjustments so that I can actually do day-to-day jobs has changed this and taken away the frustration of not being able to do things that my mum or the rest of my family can do.

For so long, I watched everyone else around me do things which, at that point, I'd only dreamed of doing; never in a million years would I have imagined that I might be able to do something like cooking and making myself pasta for dinner. But one day, after watching my mum cook me dinner innumerable times, I decided I wanted to cook dinner myself for once. Now, as I have a disability, luckily, a large number of the adjustments that have been made are to my house — and to my kitchen in particular. This means that my kitchen has a rise-and-fall oven and sink and the sides are lower as well, in case I need to use a wheelchair one day.

When the kitchen was first fitted, I didn't really use it much to try and cook and do kitchen tasks as I never thought I would be able to cook at all — even though the adjustments had been made specifically for me, so that I could be more independent. What this meant was that I didn't actually use them to their full advantage at all. And then, one day, I decided I wanted to become more independent and cook a meal for myself. So, with my mum's help and guidance, I did. I used the rise-and-fall cooker so that it would be easier for me to cook stuff on the hob, and then had my mum near at hand, just to help with a few things that I struggled with, this being my first time cooking pretty much on my own. Eventually, I cooked a meal for myself. I didn't do it all by myself, but I'd made a start at doing something that I hadn't thought I could do previously.

Years before this, if you had told me that I would need adjustments in order to do the stuff that I wanted to do, but couldn't because I was physically restricted, I would probably have told you that you were mad and that I didn't need to adjust things to make it a little bit easier for me to do them. In truth, I was very stubborn and wanted to do everything myself, in the same way that everyone else did things, because I wanted to be fully independent like other people, without needing any adjustments to be made at all.

But if I hadn't had any adjustments made to my kitchen, I would not have been able to cook myself a meal that day, because physically it would have been quite impossible for me to do in a normal kitchen. If I didn't have to live a life where I have to make adjustments all the time, that would be amazing, because it would be an easier life to live than the one I'm currently living. But I know this isn't possible, and so making adjustments is one of a small number of ways in which I can live my life with fewer barriers getting in the way. When I was first diagnosed with cerebral palsy, it was obvious that I was going to need adjustments, if I was ever going to be able to do things for myself physically. I think that, if it weren't for the adjustments that I've made or that have been made to help me, I wouldn't be as independent as I am now.

I've had adjustments made pretty much everywhere I've been — in the nursery, in school, in my home life, they have always been part of my life. I used to hate living with adjustments because I didn't like the fact that I couldn't be like everyone else and do all the things they could do in the same way they did them. I hated having to use a lift instead of walking downstairs; I hated using a laptop instead of writing by hand like all my peers; at school, I hated sitting on a chair that was different from the chairs the other students sat on. Quite simply, I hated having to make adjustments to my life to accommodate the disability I was living with. Why should I have to make adjustments to my life to deal with this terrible disability I have to live with, which is of no benefit to me at all? These were the kinds of thoughts that would go through my mind every time I had to do something differently so that I could actually do it.

The fact of the matter is that I didn't care whether these adjustments were there and had been put in place to help me. I would have preferred to suffer and be unable to do anything (which, deep down, wasn't what I wanted), rather than doing things differently so that I could be a bit more independent and do things myself unassisted. It was sad really, because I used to feel embarrassed when I had adjustments made or had to adjust to doing something differently. I felt this at school especially. Every time I had to use special equipment at school in order to help myself achieve what I wanted to achieve, I was so worried about what all the other children would think of me, and I used to be paranoid about comments being made about me behind my back. I felt I was being judged by others for using specialised equipment that was there in order to meet my needs.

Both at home and at school, I felt I had failed as a person because I couldn't do stuff in the same way as everyone else and if I did need to do something then, nine times out of ten, I would need special equipment to do it. I used to see all my family using normal cutlery at dinnertime, whilst I had to use my own specialised cutlery, and it just made me feel different. And I hated feeling different. Even nowadays, that feeling still hits me in a negative way sometimes. I guess I hated feeling like that because I've always wanted to be like everyone else and using special equipment didn't make me feel like everyone else at all. I ignored the fact that this equipment would help me in the long term and focused mainly on how it would make me look in the short term. To be honest with you, I felt that none of the equipment I was using, which was customised specifically to suit me and my needs, was cool. However, as I grew up, I realised that, no matter how old I was or where I might be in life, I was always going to need to make adjustments or have adjustments made so that I could participate in doing normal things every day, regardless of how I felt about it.

Sometimes, I just have to swallow my pride and think about how the adjustments are helping me at that very moment in time and how they will help me in the long term as well. I'm coming towards the end of my teens as I write this, and even though I've become very independent over the years and can do most things normally, I have to remember that I still have a disability which restricts me in many ways. This will always mean that, with some things, I have to make adjustments.

I realise it will always be like this, as I'm not like everyone else and not completely able-bodied like other people. So I've told myself that the adjustments aren't there in order to make you look cool, sometimes you're going to look absolutely stupid when you have to carry out certain activities in a way that's different to how everyone else does them — but so what? They're not there to make you look cool. Sure, if someone comes to your house for the very first time and sees that you've got a rise-and-fall cooker in your kitchen, maybe they'll think it's cool and that you're cool too, but that's not what these adjustments are there for. They're there to help you in life and allow you to achieve what you want to achieve, no matter how big or small the thing that you want to achieve is.

The adjustments are there to help you rather than embarrass you or make you feel small. With hindsight,

I wish I had realised all this much earlier than I did; because maybe I would've been able to do some of the things I can do now much earlier in life, if only I had just accepted the fact that adjustments will be required to help me through life. It isn't a bad thing if you have to do some things differently from how your friends or family members do them; all that matters is that you get to do the things you're aiming to do in a way that's easiest for you. Nowadays, I know it doesn't matter what anyone else thinks about how I do stuff, all that matters is that I can do things I couldn't do before and that's down to the adjustments I've made.

Chapter Thirteen

It's OK Not to Be OK

In this chapter I'm going to be honest with you about the feelings I sometimes have regarding my disability. Living with a disability is not always rainbows and flowers, sure, but I wouldn't change it for the world as it's what makes me the person I am. But this doesn't mean that I'm always loving being disabled. Being disabled can be utter crap at times and it can affect you mentally as well as physically. I've already touched on some of the low feelings I've experienced about my disability in the past and how being disabled has affected me emotionally.

If I were to say that I don't get those feelings any more and I'm completely fine about being disabled, then I would be lying. Even though I'm more accepting of my disability than I was in the past, I still have days when I absolutely hate being disabled and just wish that I was 'normal' like everyone else. When I have these days, I can feel all kinds of emotions — sadness, guilt, anger, confusion — which make that day a write-off. When I'm feeling like this, most of the time I just want to go to bed and hide away from the world. When it comes to people who are living with disabilities, I think other people just presume that we don't feel any emotions and that we're emotionless because we're disabled. They think we don't have any emotions because we're not like everyone else and don't feel all the different emotions that "normal" people experience. This is not the case at all.

Yes, I'm disabled. Yes, I'm physically different, but that doesn't mean I don't get sad or angry like everyone else, because I do, and that's OK, I'm allowed to feel like that. When I was younger, the days when I felt anger and sadness about my disability would happen a lot. All the time, actually. I think that, from very early on, I realised I didn't like my disability and didn't want to be disabled, but I couldn't change that: my disability was staying and there was nothing I could do to take it away, which made me feel worse. I used to sit and watch everyone around me being 'normal' and it would make me feel broken, as though I had something wrong with me that couldn't be fixed, and I saw myself as useless because of that. For me, being disabled was a bad thing, which would make me feel really low about myself — I felt I was bad just because I was disabled.

I hated myself for a long time. I didn't see a life full of potential for myself and couldn't even see past the next day at one point, because I felt so sad and lonely. I thought there was nothing out there for me, and I was just existing for no reason at all, without any purpose in the world. I didn't see what I could give to the world and couldn't see the experiences I might take part in. At that point, I was a burden to myself and everyone else around me.

I felt as though my only purpose on this earth was to be someone other people could bully or treat like a baby, no matter how old I was, or else they were only hanging out with me because they felt sorry for me. I didn't want to exist just for those purposes, I didn't want to be bullied or to be felt sorry for, or to be treated like a baby, I wanted to be treated like a human and be seen for the person I was and not for my disability. So, when I felt that I had little purpose in the world. I didn't want to go on any more. I nearly died when I was born and didn't see what a blessing it was to have actually survived and made it out to the other side, because this meant that, at the very start of being alive, my life wasn't guaranteed.

Sometimes, I felt so low and sorry for myself that I wished I hadn't made it to the other side and survived, because the other side was utter crap to me. Living — or, as I saw it, being trapped — in a body, in which you constantly ached and were restricted in what you could do, was so hard to deal with. Knowing that you'd never be able to experience all the things that your able-bodied friends could experience and already had done was a smack in the face. I felt robbed of the life that I should have been living, a life that all my friends were living.

It feels a bit like after a house has been robbed — the house feels much emptier than it did before it was robbed. Because I have never lived without a disability, I think I'm like that house except that, in my case, I've always been empty, and so there's nothing to rob. I think there were so many facets about my disability that led to me seeing it as a terrible thing, and they contributed to the big toll it took on my mental health: not being accepted by the outside world, not feeling like you belong anywhere, feeling like an alien in the world. All these things had an impact on me and they made me feel as really low.

After years of experiencing all these negative emotions and feeling trapped in a body that I didn't want, I hated life in general and thought to myself, "Why would I want to live this life when it has been so unfair to me by giving me this disability? What do I owe life by living it?". I never saw the beauty in life at all, only the darkness and how unfair it was that everybody else was 'normal' and I wasn't. I felt I was being punished for something but didn't know exactly what I was being punished for. I really wanted to be happy and enjoy life, but I couldn't because I was disabled which, for me, was such a bad thing and hard to live with at times as well.

Life seemed so unfair to me for so many reasons and all the reasons led back to my disability. Since realising how I felt for so many years, it has been hard for me to see that it wasn't normal to have all those feelings of hatred towards myself and the world because I felt them for so long; those negative emotions became normal to me, and in my eyes, it was normal to feel that way. But then, one day, it dawned on me that I was in a dark place and that I had been there for a long time. I realised it wasn't normal to hate myself for something I couldn't help or control and to wake up every day wishing the day was already over, so that I didn't have to face the world with this disability clinging to me, pulling me down. When I started speaking up about how I felt, my family and friends agreed it wasn't normal to feel like this all the time, so I spoke to an independent person about how I was feeling.

For such a long time, I didn't appreciate my worth at all. I thought that I was completely worthless, both to myself and the world around me. So when I spoke to this other person and my family and friends and told them how I felt about everything, it made me realise that it wasn't normal to feel that way. I shouldn't hate myself or feel down and gloomy about the world around me — feeling like that isn't normal in any way at all. I think the hardest thing at that point, when I started to speak up about how I was feeling, was recognising that I felt so low because I didn't accept my disability. I wanted to make out that it wasn't a case of hating my disability — my disability wasn't the problem at all — , but deep down, I knew this wasn't true, my disability was exactly the problem.

Getting upset about how the world treated me at times or why I wasn't normal, was all down to me not accepting the fact that I was disabled and different to everyone else. But with the help and support of my family and friends, I had to accept that this was the reason for all the low feelings inside me at that time. In order to feel better, I needed to admit that this was all down to me not accepting myself. This was very hard as I felt like a failure for admitting that I wasn't OK; I thought I was weak, but I was the opposite.

Speaking up made me realise how strong I actually was, being able to admit that I wasn't OK and needed help. It made me realise my worth and recognise all the good aspects of my disability, not the bad aspects. I was finally able to accept a part of myself that I wouldn't have done previously. It was good knowing that I could now see positive things about myself, after spending so long seeing mainly bad things and putting myself down in so many ways. You could say I felt free because I wasn't being dragged down by all those negative emotions.

However, as I said before, this doesn't mean that my life is all rainbows and flowers, or that I never feel low about myself or my disability or that I'm happy all the time, when these things aren't true. I still face demons because of being disabled; some days I hate the fact that I'm different; I still loathe being disabled at times and prefer not to face the future living with a disability. Even though I have come to accept my disability a lot more than in the past, living with a disability is crap on some days, and on those days, I wish I didn't have it, because it can be a pain up the backside. I can't sit here and say I love being disabled every second of every day, because the truth is that I don't.

But do you know what? It's OK. It's OK to feel all these emotions towards my disability because it's hard, really hard at times, to the point where I just want to give up on everything I've ever achieved or worked towards. Over the years, I've realised that it's part of life to feel like this, as though the whole world is against you. You can't be happy all the time, you wouldn't be human if that were the case.

I've got a disability. But I've got feelings and emotions as well, which affect me at times. I also know that I'm only human and that this is all part of the cycle of life. Being human isn't easy, especially if you're like me and have a disability as well, but I'm willing to battle through the hard times of being disabled in order to get to the good times, because there are so many things you can give the world. I wish I had told myself this all those years ago when I hated being disabled and felt like the whole world was against me. At the same time, though, I'm glad I went through all that and felt those emotions, because I am where I am mentally today because of those past experiences.

Chapter Fourteen

Wanting to Live an Independent Life

Independence is a big thing for me. As someone who was told that they'll never walk or talk, pretty much from the get-go, I have always craved independence. In some areas I have independence but in other areas I don't have as much, which is difficult for me, as I want to be like everyone else and do all the things that someone without a disability does.

In day-to-day life, I see people behaving independently all the time and I try to be like them, being as independent as I possibly can, but this is easier said than done. Every day I wake up wanting to do everything myself, without help from anyone around me, and at times I even forget that I have a disability as I try and get on with my life. And sometimes, I forget all about the risks involved in trying to do the things that everyone else does in their daily lives — but with a disability.

So, when I go to make a hot drink or cook a meal there's always a greater risk for me in doing these things than there is for anyone else in my family. But in my mind, when I want to cook a meal or make a hot drink, I don't think about the risks involved as much, what's uppermost in my mind is thinking "If I do this then I'm a little bit closer to being fully independent like my parents and siblings are". I choose not to think about the risks as much as I probably should.

I've said before that asking for help wasn't really an option for me when I was younger, and to be honest, it still isn't always an option. I hate asking for help because I'm stubborn, it makes me feel I'm more disabled than I actually am, and I hate the feeling of being less independent because I'm asking other people to help with certain jobs that I find a struggle. Every time I ask for help, I always feel I'm relying on others too much, so I avoid asking for help as much as possible.

But here's the thing, when I'm struggling with something such as tying up a shoelace or making a drink, asking for help is sometimes my only option whether I want help or not — without help I wouldn't get very far with doing stuff. And I've realised that everyone asks for help sometimes; it doesn't mean they're not independent and can't do anything for themselves. But at some points in everyone's lives, we all need a bit of help and can't do everything by ourselves, and there's nothing wrong with that.

Even though asking for help was a big issue for me, I've come to terms with the fact that I need more help than others. It doesn't mean I'm a failure or any less of a person, I just need more help sometimes, that's all. As I've said before, I'd rather do things myself, but this is easier said than done. I can't just make myself a cup of tea at the first attempt because, if I did, I'd be potentially putting myself at risk of being burnt by boiling water.

Everything I want to do to be able to live an independent life comes with practice. I need to practise those day-to-day jobs most people find easy, so that I'll be able to do them in future. When I do practise doing day-to-day activities, it means I can figure out what I struggle with when carrying out each activity and what special equipment I might need to help me succeed in doing simple jobs, making them easier for me to do. So, when I next attempt a job that I've practised doing in the past, I'll know what equipment is needed and I'll be able to do it.

During my lifetime, I might not be able to do all the things my mum and dad can do. I might not be able to carry a hot drink in one hand without spilling it or lift a heavy pan with hot food in it. Sometimes, when I think about what I might not be able to do, occasionally it gets me down because the realisation of being different comes to mind, making me wonder if this will stop me from being independent.

In the future, I hope to be able to live independently, so being able to do certain jobs and getting adaptable equipment that will enable me to live on my own is really important, so that I can achieve this dream. I don't want to be reliant on other people to do stuff for me, it makes me feel like a child, and nobody wants to feel they're being treated like a child. I certainly don't. I want to be able to do things by myself and do everything unassisted. I don't want help. But I also know that I'm going to need *some* help in the future, whether it's a carer who comes and does the cooking for me or something else.

Some people might like the thought of someone coming into their household and doing everything for them but I hate it. In my eyes, living an independent life doesn't involve someone coming in and doing chores for you, that's not being independent. Being independent is doing your own chores and not relying on someone else to do them. But it's not that simple for me. Unfortunately, having someone who comes in to cook or clean may become reality for me one day. I may need that kind of help because I might not be able to cook substantial meals and I may struggle with hoovering under sofas.

Getting someone to help in the future isn't ever *not* going to be an option for me. I'm quite reluctant about facing up to this, but over time, I've come to accept that help will be available and that I'll always need it at some point in my life. Whether I'm in my twenties or my eighties, help will always be there for me. But there is one thing that's stopping me from accepting help at present and may stop me in the future — and that's my stubbornness. I don't like asking for help because I'm stubborn, as I've said before, but it's not just because I want to be independent, it's because I want to feel grown up.

When you're very young, you rely on your parents and carers to do simple tasks for you, such as tying up shoelaces or making a drink, because you're too small to do it yourself. Well, I'm a teenager, and even though I may be disabled, I'm not a little kid any more; but sometimes I still need someone to tie up my shoelaces or make me a drink because activities like these can be too physically demanding for me. Mentally, however, this makes me feel as though I'm still a little kid who can't do anything for herself and is generally pretty useless.

I don't want to feel like a kid. I want to feel like a teenager who's independent and does things for herself and has no need to rely on anyone else to do stuff for her. Even though I can do most things for myself, there are still some things I need help with, and no matter how I feel about that, in the long run it will be beneficial. I need to keep telling myself this, that's the thing, instead of simply turning help down just because it makes me appear less independent and lazy.

As teens, we're often lazy and don't really do anything for ourselves, mainly relying on our parents to do everything for us. We'd rather be out with our friends doing whatever than staying at home doing household chores that our mums will do for us. Seen this way, we teens are quite literally slobs — I bet you 99% of us have messy rooms with stuff all over the place. If you were to enter, there would be absolutely no carpet to walk on, as the room would be that messy. This is a typical teenager's life, having messy rooms, not helping around the house and doing chores, and simply being lazy.

Now, because I have a disability, I feel as though I can't be lazy in the slightest and so I do help my mum out by doing chores around the house. This is all because the chores that my mum does, such as cleaning or doing the washing, are the kinds of things that I will have to do if I want to live an independent life in the future. So, by doing the household chores, I'm not only helping my mum out with stuff, I'm teaching myself how to do these chores, whilst my mum is there to teach me how to do other chores, to correct me if I do things wrong and to give me advice on jobs such as how to use the dishwasher.

Normal teens would be able to move into adulthood and be fully independent, just like that, after years of not doing chores on a daily basis. It's a natural thing for them when eventually the time comes for them to become adults. It isn't that simple for me. So, by learning how to do daily chores now, while I have the chance to get help and advice from my parents on doing them, I'm kind of training myself to be able to live independently by practising doing things that most teens wouldn't need to practise as much as I do before they can live independently.

When I grow up, I dream of living a fully independent life, a life that many people in the world take for granted — they don't even give it a second thought because they have the advantage of living their lives independently. For me, achieving this dream is going to be difficult, but I'm determined to achieve it no matter how hard it will be.

That's why doing all this, practising certain household day-to-day jobs at the age I am now and accepting help when I need it, is important for me because doing this will help me get closer to achieving my dream. In my eyes, life is way too short to be sitting around and not doing anything with your life, and that's why it's important for me to achieve what I want to achieve in my lifetime, including living independently.

For me, living independently means that I can fulfil things in life, not just normal household chores but other activities such as going travelling and seeing the world, or going to university and getting a degree. These are things I could do easily whilst living an independent life. I don't want to give up on my dreams because, physically, my body won't allow me to realise them; I want to realise my dreams and stop my disability from getting in the way of doing that.

I know I won't be as able-bodied as my siblings are when we're older and I might not be able to do some of the things they'll be able to do. I have to find a way of coming to terms with this, but I'm determined to get the life I want to live and to live independently, regardless of my disability and the struggles that will come with it. I know this will be hard for me to achieve, but I'm resolved to get through every struggle that comes with it, in order to be able to live the independent life I so want.

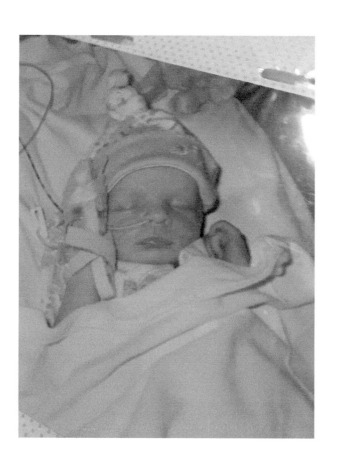

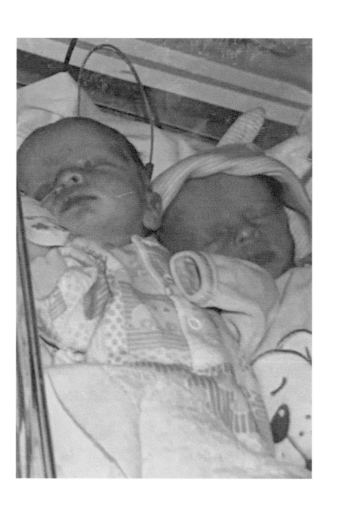

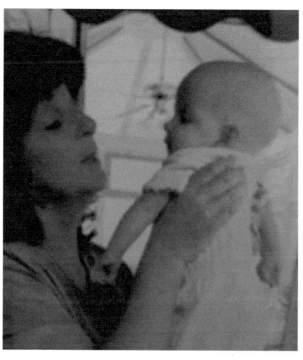

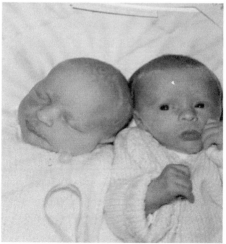

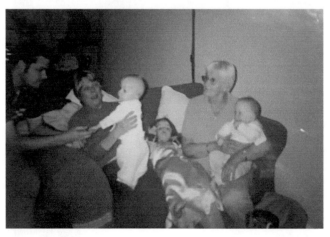

Chapter Fifteen

What Actually is Normal?

1 hate the word "normal". What does it actually mean? What is it? As a society, we appear to see individuals who are perfectly able-bodied and have nothing about them that the outside world would find peculiar as 'normal'. But is that really what "normal" means, or is that just how the world and society have influenced us into thinking this is the meaning of "normal"? As a disabled person, I have certainly not been seen as normal at various points in my life and that's down to society's perceptions of disability. You see, because I'm not able-bodied like most other people, I don't fit very well into the category of "normal" and so, because of this, at times people see me as rather peculiar. However, that may not be the case at all, and I may not fit within the category of "normal" because of my weird personality and my habit of laughing at absolutely nothing — I don't quite know.

I've mentioned before that this has sometimes affected the way I'm seen by others, and I think it's very clear that, when something or someone is not "normal" to us, we put it down as a negative instead of a positive. So when someone hasn't seen or doesn't see me as "normal", I'm viewed in a negative light, and I get treated differently or even badly at times. You see, we're all different, nobody's the same, we've all got differently coloured hair, differently coloured eyes, different skin colours or tones. But it's funny that, when it comes to the differences in how someone looks, if a person doesn't have a disability or infirmity, then the features I've listed above aren't usually seen as "different". However, when it comes to disabilities, such people are labelled as "different" all the time and are often also seen in a negative light.

This is because, as I've said, differences are often associated with negativity. If someone happened to have brown hair and another person had blonde hair, you would think they're equivalent, as they have all the features they should have and can do all the things they should be able to do as humans. However, if someone had brown hair and another person had blonde hair but also had a disability, you would think the person with blonde hair was different, and no, it wouldn't be because they had blonde hair and the other person had brown hair, it would be because the person with blonde hair has a disability. In that scenario, you wouldn't say they're the same and that would be because a disability has been thrown into the mix.

It doesn't matter what you look like, if you have something resembling a disability, then you are automatically condemned as not being 'normal' just because you have a disability. I hate the fact that I've been seen that way because of having a disability. So now I'm not normal, just because I have a disability? Not because I have blonde hair and blue eyes or wear leggings, but simply because I'm living with a disability?

We're so used to seeing what's "normal" as a good thing that we don't celebrate all the differences there are around the world that much. We've been duped into thinking this and how great it is to be "normal", so when someone is "different", they're automatically frowned on by others. There have been times when this has affected me massively and made me question my disability. Why is it such a bad thing that I'm not seen as "normal" in the world around me? Why has it become such an issue? Because that's how it's seen by people when they see others with disabilities. I find this is the case anyway, as I've experienced being seen as "a problem" simply because I'm disabled. I get that disability isn't great, especially living with it, but why then should people all over the world living with disability be seen as "different" and "problematic" as well?

I've been stared at many times, I've been called horrible names, I've had all sorts of things happen to me, just because I'm disabled. For me, the world has got so wound up about how differences and disabilities are such a bad thing that it's taken this out on the people who are living with these differences and disabilities. We get the brunt of how not being 'normal' is viewed by the world. In a way, it's as though we're the issue and have committed a crime when, actually, the only "crime" we've ever committed is simply being born different. We're not how a "perfect" human should be, we're not that "normal" person who is part of the world because they are that way. That's so unfair! Why are we being punished for something we can't help, for not being "perfect" (which, by the way, no one is), for not being "normal"? I may not be seen as "normal" to society and the people within it, but I am human, I have a heart, I have a brain, I have feelings. But just because I have a disability which makes me somehow physically different, I am automatically seen in a negative light by so many people.

I sometimes wonder what the world would be like if "normality" didn't exist at all, how much more equality there would be in it, and how everyone would be treated the same and seen as equals. I think the world would be a much better place if that were the case; no one would ever feel left out or made to feel they're a bad person because of who they are. This vision of how the world might be would have been ideal for me, growing up with a disability. I wouldn't have had to experience all those feelings of being left out and seen as a bad person. Life would have been so much easier in so many ways, if only the concept of "normal" didn't exist. What a kinder world it would be if there were no distinctions like "normal".

I don't know why there is a criterion such as "normal" in this world; for the seventeen years that I've been on this earth, I've tried to figure out what it actually means to be "normal". I've even tried to make myself "normal" at times but have never really succeeded because I don't know what "normal" actually means — and never have, even to this day.

To me, the word "normal" is such crap. It's just a term that someone made up thousands of years ago and then it was used to refer to a load of people who liked it, and it went from there. That's how I see it — it's just a random word that some random person made up and then everyone else got conditioned by it, and 'normal' became the way to be from then on. I think that if "normal" hadn't been created and spread around the world all those years ago, then it wouldn't be such a big deal nowadays.

I don't know why "normal" was created. There shouldn't even be such a thing as "normal"; people should be accepted in the world and in society exactly for who they are. People shouldn't feel embarrassed about who they are or feel the need to hide themselves from the world. I have felt like this so many times when people have judged me for being different and not "normal". Whenever I meet new people, the first thing that stands out for them is that I'm different. Most of the time, they see that as something negative and that leads them to give me a frosty reception. I think that's why I've always struggled with making friends in my life, because of my disability and being different from everyone else. This is then portrayed as being "a bad thing".

There's never been a time at school or at college when I've met someone my age and we've hit it off straight away and become friends: that never happens. Most of the time, the opposite happens, and I'm either ignored or not included in things, and that's because I'm different and not "normal". On many occasions, I've felt angry because of this. I'm a good person who tries to be kind to everyone I come across, but my disability and people's views on it conceal this and so I'm seen as "the disabled one". People get uncomfortable with this, because it isn't "normal" for them to be meeting someone who has a disability — they're out of their comfort zone.

But it shouldn't be like that. People shouldn't be in a comfort zone inhabited by "normal" people because that zone lacks diversity and equality which, in my eyes, are two important things. If we were to start teaching people, especially children, about diversity and everything else out there that helps to make the world a fairer place for everyone — no matter who they are, then just maybe the label "normal" wouldn't be such a big thing for people. In this world, labels wouldn't exist and everyone would be seen as equal, instead of some people being excluded for not being like everyone else.

I feel that, over time, people have come to realise that no one is "normal". Everyone is different. We don't actually know what "normal" means, we just label people as "normal" for whatever reason and we don't really know what that reason is. We're just following the traditions of past generations by labelling some people as "normal" and others as "not normal".

But we don't have to do that, and differences should be celebrated instead of being frowned on, no matter what they are. We're all people, physically we're all the same as we have human bodies, so surely that should be enough for people to come together and realise that it doesn't matter who's "normal" or who's "different"? We're all human and surely that should be enough for "normality" to be forgotten about.

What is "normal"? Why does it even exist? I ask myself these questions all the time and I don't think they will ever be answered because none of us knows what "normal" is. No one is "normal" in my eyes, everyone's different, and that's not a bad thing at all. Each of us is unique and that should be seen as a good thing, not a bad thing. None of us are "normal", but we are all human, so we deserve to be treated equally and seen as equals too.

Chapter Sixteen

Wanting What Other People Have in Life

As a little girl, when I grew up to be an adult, I didn't want to be a fairy princess or an astronaut or anything extreme: that was what everyone else wanted from life. Instead, what I wanted was the same as what happens to a lot of girls: I wanted to be a wife, for someone who would love me for who I am and then to become a mum one day. I wanted that fairy-tale ending everyone else wants, and to this day, it has always been my dream. But I know that, of all my dreams, this will probably be the hardest to achieve, if it is ever achieved.

If you're reading this, some of you guys are probably married with kids, so this may be such a small thing to dream about because it's the norm for you guys: lots of people get married and have kids all the time. But when you're not abled-bodied, this dream is something you can only imagine and you can't think of it actually coming true for you. Let me explain why this is. In order to get married, you need to meet someone. But that someone can't be just anyone, it has to be someone who loves you for who you are and with whom you feel a connection. The person you marry is usually the one for you, after you've kissed a load of frogs — as the saying goes, you need to kiss a few frogs before you meet your prince. Now, in my seventeen years of living, I haven't yet managed to kiss a boy, let alone get a boyfriend. But that's probably music to my mum and dad's ears!

I know it's very rare, in this day and age and while in your teens, to meet someone who's the one for you and then go on to marry them and have kids. The people you might form romantic relationships with initially will probably turn into frogs in the future (your ex-partners). But the thing is, for me, I haven't even met my first frog yet so, in my view, it's going to be a while before I meet my prince — if I ever meet him. I need to kiss a few frogs first, unless I'm extremely lucky and my prince is the first person I kiss. And because I haven't had a boyfriend or kissed a boy, like most girls of my age have done, it makes me feel as though I'll never meet "the one"; from my point of view, if nobody has wanted me as a girlfriend in the past, why would anyone want me as one in the future? What will change then?

You may think I'm presuming that all this is down to me being disabled; and trust me, it is indeed down to me being disabled. Most of the time anyway. You see, in the past, I have tried asking boys out and tried to get myself a boyfriend, but whenever I've asked a boy to be my boyfriend, most of the time they say no, and the reason for this is that I'm disabled. I've even been told this by some of them. For many reasons, I was desperate to get a boyfriend at school, to experience what it would be like to be loved romantically, to be like everyone else who was in a relationship, but mainly to confirm in my own mind that I could actually get a boyfriend. I didn't want to worry about not getting married at a future date, due to my lack of success in trying to get a boy to like me.

I used to ask my best friend if her boyfriend had any friends I could try and be with because I was that desperate to confirm it wasn't me who was the reason why I couldn't get a boyfriend. I didn't want to think it was me and my disability that were the main problem and why boys didn't seem to like me in a romantic way. But I knew, deep down, that my disability was the issue. I think it's hard enough for people of my age or in their teens to accept disabilities, because they are seen as such a negative thing to them, so being friends with someone who has a disability might be embarrassing at times. I didn't want to think about how a boy would feel dating a girl like me with a disability.

At one time, there was a boy I really liked who was in my year at school, and over time, I started to wonder what it would be like if we were in a relationship — whatever a relationship might be at that age. I told my friends at the time, and we came to an arrangement that, at break-time one day, on my behalf, they were going to ask this boy if he wanted to go out with me. In the lead-up to that day, I was really excited about potentially getting a boyfriend at last. So, when the day came, and on my behalf, my friends were going to ask him out, my nerves were all over the place. Will he say yes? Will he say no? Will he laugh at the thought of me going out with him? Does he fancy me like I fancy him? This was all ridiculous as I was twelve-years-old at the time and didn't even know what real love was — so why was I getting myself all worked up about this kind of thing?

Anyway, I watched my friends go to where he was standing with his friends and I saw them ask him out for me and then walk back. As they were walking back, I could see him with his friends laughing and smirking in the background, and I just knew, judging by their reactions, the answer was "no". Then my friends came and confirmed it was "no" as well. I felt heartbreak for the rest of that day and thought no one would ever want me, and that sense of being unwanted romantically has stuck with me until now. I see people get into relationships, get engaged, get married and have kids, and initially, I feel really happy for them as it's lovely to see people getting together. But then there's a kind of jealousy and sadness deep down inside me, as though I already know those things are never going to happen to me because I'm disabled.

Social media is a real pain in this connection as it paints a perfect picture of life, especially about couples and engagements and relationships, when usually there's a reality behind the picture which isn't as perfect as social media makes it out to be. So why do I still experience these feelings of jealousy and sadness when I know this is the case — life isn't how it comes across on social media? It's because I still want these things in the future, even though, at this moment in time, I'm not desperate for a relationship like I used to be and I'm certainly not ready to have kids. But this doesn't mean that, some day in the future, I wouldn't want to experience and have the things that come to most people.

In some ways, I let my past predict my future. In my mind, I'm thinking I've never had a boyfriend and so why would I ever have one in the future, let alone get married to my 'soulmate'? There are so many people telling me not to be negative about love and that there's 'someone for everyone'. I often think to myself, "Really, is there really someone out there for me?", but that may just be me being negative and maybe there is someone out there for me — I hope so anyway. Maybe I just need to be patient — and I am — because I'm not even looking for love any more. As sad as it might sound, I've pretty much given up on it at my present age, which may be stupid, but I don't want to raise my hopes of finding "the one" and then find those hopes are crushed.

I don't want to dream about having what an able-bodied person might have and then expect that to happen to me, when in fact I'm disabled and not like an able-bodied person at all. I guess, as I don't expect to get married, I don't expect to have kids either. I've always wanted to be a mum and remember, from a young age, playing with baby dolls all the time and I loved being around babies as well. I've always had a maternal instinct, wanting to be a mum and have kids. To my mind, it would be absolutely awesome to have mini versions of ME running around.

Again, this is only a dream. I don't expect it to become reality because I'm disabled. First, before I actually have kids of my own, I need to find Mr Right, and as I've stated a few times in this chapter, I'm not expecting to meet him at all. I'm not yet an adult, but when I look at baby clothes in the shops, I feel this sadness. But then there's no need for me to feel this sadness, as I'm still a teenager and definitely not ready to have a baby yet. But the sadness is there because I fear I'll never be going into shops to buy baby clothes for my own baby. This hurts deep down already, especially knowing I'll have to watch everyone else who's close to me and around my age get married and have babies. I feel this is going to be hard for me, perhaps selfishly, because seeing your friends or your siblings have babies, when that's all you want but can't have, is really tough.

Some people don't have kids with their "soulmates" and some parents break up, but in my head, I've told myself I won't have kids with someone unless they're "the one" for me. But because I don't think there's anyone out there for me, I don't think I'm going to have kids. It pains me that I think like this, as I've never let my disability get in the way of my other dreams, but with this one, it's kind of in the way. And yet again, that's down to how society sees disabilities; and so, men won't want to be with a woman like me because she's disabled.

This shouldn't be the case and I know I shouldn't feel like this because, even though I'm disabled, I am worth that kind of love and to be loved unconditionally by a man one day. Someone suggested that there are alternative ways to have a baby and I wouldn't need to be with anyone in order to have children, but that's not the point: yeah, I want children, but I want children with *someone*, and I'd like to experience marriage as well. I don't know why I feel so negative about love and having children. I guess I've never come across anyone who has cerebral palsy and has gone on to get married and have children, someone I could look up to and who could be a role model for me.

Because I don't have a role model, it makes me wonder whether I can get married and have children, because I've never seen someone with the same disability as me who has gone on to do that. I hope that, one day, I can be a role model for young girls who, like me, have completely given up on love and everything that comes with it, so that fewer girls will feel the way I do right now, that there's no one out there for them. I hate the fact that I'm slowly giving up on the dream of becoming a wife and a mum simply because I'm disabled and feel that, for me, this dream is too good to be true. But then again, I must be more positive about life and what it has to offer.

I can't just give up on my dreams because that's letting my disability win, and I don't want that. So, to keep positive, I tell myself this: I hope, one day, I'll find a man who will love and accept me for exactly who I am and who will want to marry me and spend the rest of their life with me. For that reason, I hope to have children of my own and be the best mum I possibly can be for them and teach them all the things that my mum and dad have taught me. I hope I don't give up on this dream completely, as it's something I've always wanted in life, and I'm not willing to let my disability get in the way of it. Deep down, I know there is someone out there for me. I just need to be patient and wait for him and wait for the other things that might arise from meeting him.

Chapter Seventeen

Appointments

As individuals, in general, we go to doctors' appointments occasionally. But speaking as someone with a disability, I must say that doctors' appointments — and other appointments that have nothing to do with doctors — have been around most of my life and have been part of it for quite some time now. When I was a baby, as I've said before, I wasn't developing at the same pace as my twin brother and other babies of my age. Because of this, I had to go to more doctors' appointments than most babies to find out what was wrong with me and whether the circumstances of my birth were linked to me not developing properly; at the time, the doctors and specialists believed this was the case. But after monthly doctors' appointments for the first year of my life, neither doctors nor specialists could put a finger on what was causing me not to develop properly, and nobody knew whether I had a disability or not.

But then, when I was about fourteen months old, my family received the diagnosis that I had cerebral palsy. After we got this diagnosis at last, we didn't quite know how many appointments would lie ahead of me, and we just had to take it one day at a time. From a young age, I was already going to doctors' appointments, physio appointments and loads of other appointments. At every one, the doctors — or whoever I was having an appointment with — were trying to figure out how the cerebral palsy was affecting me and what I could or couldn't do.

It was hard because, from a very young age, I couldn't be a normal kid. I couldn't go to playgroups on the days when I had these appointments, and on some days, instead of playing in the park with other kids of my age, I was playing with the toys in the hospital waiting room as I waited to be seen by a doctor about whether I needed this or that. That became normality for me sometimes. I wasn't like any other kid and only dreamed of having the privileges that other kids of my age enjoyed.

I didn't really understand why, amongst my siblings and peers, I was the only one who had to go to doctors' appointments and physio sessions and see all kinds of specialists, while they got to go to the park and to parties. I would sometimes wonder what was wrong with me and why they didn't go to doctors' appointments, and I remember begging my mum to let me go to the park instead of going to do physio. But unfortunately on some days that couldn't happen.

As I got older and had to miss school because it was necessary to see a specialist or some other medical expert, sometimes I'd be happy about missing school because school could be quite boring at times; but then, at other times, I'd feel lonely and jealous of all my classmates as they could be normal kids and stay in school, whilst I had to go to hospitals, therapy centres and other places. Normally, most kids would be excited about missing school but it's different when you miss school because of something that's wrong with you.

When I was younger, these appointments took place a lot more often than they do now, which is a good thing, as I can just get on with life and don't have to worry about making plans around physio sessions or paediatric assessments. But back then, I had to attend more speech, language and physio sessions, and so most of what I did in my life had to revolve around these sessions and other appointments at various times. I can recall, when I was little, one appointment was about getting orthotics to make my feet stronger when I was walking. I remember this one specifically because the doctors were shaping plaster around my feet and I remember how cool it was watching them make these orthotics. But I also remember having to wear them in my shoes all the time when I walked, and to be honest, they weren't really cool then.

Not only were they uncomfortable but no one else wore them. Even though I thought it was quite satisfying to see how the orthotics were made and watching them plaster my feet to shape the orthotics felt weird but nice, having to wear them every day wasn't cool or nice at all. I didn't like the fact that I was the only one who had to wear them. But as time went on, even though I didn't realise it, the orthotics helped my walking a lot and so did going to physio sessions. As I was too young at the time, it didn't really matter whether wearing the orthotics was fashionable or not — they weren't made for that — I just didn't like the way it felt walking in them or that I was the only one who had to walk around wearing them. But they helped me a lot physically, and fortunately, after a period of time spent wearing them, the doctors eventually said I didn't have to wear them any more.

The result of wearing the orthotics was that my walking wasn't as bad as it was before I started wearing them, which was a good thing. But at the time, I found it really irritating going to all these appointments and having to get special aids that I needed to wear but no one else wore. It was good going to appointments but hard at the same time, especially the ones at the hospital where I had to be assessed. It made me wonder if they were assessing me as a person and whether I was good enough for the world because I had a disability. I know that's stupid, but at times, because nobody else had to have these assessments made, I used to think this way.

Even though I didn't like hospital appointments, I didn't mind the physio appointments as much. Although sometimes I had to take time out of my day and not make plans with family or friends because I had to go to these appointments, I actually found physio sessions quite fun at times.

Sometimes I'd be involved in doing activities with the therapist, which I quite liked as I found them really fun. It didn't seem as if I was doing physio and working on my physical wellbeing, and even though I wasn't playing with toys or in parks with the other kids, for me, doing physio was playing in a way. Sometimes, that's how I saw it, having the time of my life trying to balance on a big round ball. It was a bonus for me when this happened because, not only would I be having fun doing what I was doing, but some of the exercises and delicate motor activities I did were helping me to get stronger and preventing cerebral palsy from controlling my body.

But then there were other times when I hated physiotherapy and didn't find it fun at all: I simply didn't want to do it and just wanted to be like all the other kids. At times, I wouldn't see it as playing; it was more like a therapy that was taking me away from my childhood and trying to control my life, which I didn't like. To be honest, I felt like this sometimes because I was too tired, and at other times it was because I wanted to be like everyone else, not do any therapy at all, and go to the playground instead.

I just wanted to stop going to all these physio sessions and other appointments and wanted everyone to forget I had a disability. I knew deep down that the appointments were there to help me, but to bring some normality into being a kid, I didn't want help if it meant I couldn't be normal and enjoy the same life as others. As sad as it might sound, I was so desperate to be like others that I would have preferred to let my body deteriorate, in an effort to try and be 'normal', rather than keep the appointments I needed to attend.

But I didn't have a choice. I couldn't just not attend appointments because nobody else did, because nobody else had a disability. I had to attend them. If I didn't, then my cerebral palsy would have got the better of me and been in control of my life, and I didn't want that. But I hated having to come away from my normal day-to-day life and take time out of my day because of the stupid disability I was living with.

In my mind, I thought the disability was never going to go away, so what was the point of all these stupid appointments that were a waste of time? They were never going to get rid of my disability, they were never going to make me normal like everyone else, they were just meaningless and taking time out of my day.

And sometimes when I felt my life was revolving around appointments and physiotherapy, I just wanted to give up. Did people only see my disability when they saw me? Was I never going to be seen as Issy, a girl who just wants to get on and live her life as best she can? I remember feeling so angry, thinking that cerebral palsy was controlling my life. It was making sure it was there and being spoken about, that's what all the appointments were for, to make sure cerebral palsy was there and taking up space in my mind, getting in the way of my life.

But as I've become older, I realise that appointments are going to be part of my life, regardless of whether I like them or not, they're going to be there. But they're not there for my cerebral palsy; they're there so that I can tackle cerebral palsy and prevent it from getting in the way of what I want to achieve in my life.

And even though taking time out of my day to go to all these appointments is a pain up the backside, I need to accept that doctors' appointments, physio sessions and other appointments will always play a big part in my life and they are helping me to succeed. I will always have to attend them because, if I don't, my cerebral palsy will get the upper hand and try to bring me down.

Along my journey with cerebral palsy, every appointment I've been to and every therapist, specialist or doctor I've met during all these appointments have helped me stop this from happening. So, because of that, in a way, I value the doctors' and physio and speech appointments. Even now it's hard, but I'm willing to do whatever is necessary to avoid letting cerebral palsy get in my way.

Chapter Eighteen

Things I Struggle With and will Continue to Struggle With

We're all doing things every single day of our lives, from the day we're born to the day we die, no matter how big or small they are. And let's be honest, people don't think about things they do from day to day, they don't really see them as a privilege. But I do because, once upon a time, the thought of me being able to do things for myself was uncertain.

But over time that changed. "Uncertain" became "certain" as I was learning new things and how to do them for myself, and soon enough, I became more independent. But I wasn't fully independent like my siblings and peers, and I'm still not. As you probably all know by now, I'm restricted in what I can or can't do and I can't do all the things that everyone else around me can do.

Every day of my life, I have to think before I tackle certain jobs, no matter how big or small they are. I have to find a way of doing these jobs that makes them easier and less of a struggle for me. I can't do them in the way everyone else does them because it's either too hard or too risky for me to do it their way. And sometimes it's impossible for me to do the job because it's too hard and there's simply no way I can do it, so I either have to leave it or ask for help.

Not being able to do certain things for myself or others is frustrating because I want to be independent. But I know there will be certain things I won't be able to do, and when I come across them, I will probably be frustrated with myself, whatever the job is. But even though I can't do everything, I know that feeling frustrated isn't the answer.

For the rest of my life, I will always struggle to do stuff that other people may be able to do, and I know this will affect my life in various ways. For instance, going into adulthood with a disability will be hard for me. Becoming an adult is quite exciting for many people, but for me, it's a worry and something I'm quite nervous about. I will have to think about what equipment I'm going to need so that I can be independent when doing certain jobs, but I'll also need to think about what I won't be able to do as I go through life.

For many, they probably don't have to think about this sort of stuff or worry as much. They can probably plan their futures to be as they want them to be and will be able to follow their dreams. They won't have to relate them to potential limitations as they're doing so. For me, it's a little different.

I have dreams and I can plan the future, but sometimes I have to take a step back and consider whether I'll be able to carry out these plans or not. And every plan I make has to revolve around my disability. That's annoying because I have loads of plans which I want to bring to fruition, but which will probably be hard to execute, or else I won't be able to achieve them at all because I'm disabled.

I think about my future and what I might struggle with all the time. Sometimes I even get upset about it as I'm thinking about how I won't be able to do certain things. At other times, I wish I was a little girl again, so that I wouldn't have to worry about this. But then people tell me to focus on the *now*. Focus on what you want to get better at *now*. So that's what I do, I forget about future worries, and try to get better at the exercises I'm struggling with now.

Whether it's cooking or styling my hair, I've learnt that, if I want to be successful with what I want to do in life, I need to give myself a kick up the backside and solve what I'm struggling with at this moment in time, so that I can do it without a struggle in the future. It can be difficult and frustrating when I'm trying to get better at what I'm finding hard to do, as sometimes I still fail to do it. It makes me feel worthless and angry because I can't succeed in doing stuff that everyone else can do.

Not being able to do certain things is hard emotionally as well as physically. I want to be fully independent in life and not need help with anything, so not being able to do stuff for myself means I'm further away from that fully independent life I dream of. It's the normal day-to-day things that I struggle with (and possibly will in the future) which gets to me the most, such as tying a shoelace, making a cup of tea, cooking, styling my hair and many more activities. These things are easy for others to do but not for me.

People do these things every day of their lives, and as I've said, they probably don't give it a second thought and just do them; in a way, I find this so unfair. Why can't I do jobs like that really easily? And of course, I know the answer to this question, but it doesn't take away the anger I feel when I fail in trying to do the jobs that everyone else can do, while knowing why I can't do these jobs or struggle to do them.

It doesn't matter how old I get, what I do with my life, or where I go, there will always be things that I'll find difficult to do for the rest of my life. It won't be easy and in some cases it will be very hard, but the only option I have is to carry on with life and face these struggles.

No matter how hard it gets, that's the only way forward. Giving up on life isn't an option and never will be, no matter how hard I find things. That's hopefully what I'll have at the back of my mind every time life gets difficult and my disability gets in the way. It will remind me that I can do it when there is stuff that is harder for me to do and I can get past these difficult times. I have an idea of what some of this stuff might be.

As we grow up, we become more independent. We become employers, parents; we become loads of things, and this will be a walk in the park for most people, but not for me. Taking on new roles such as being a parent is hard for anyone, but when you add disability into the mix, having a new role in life is even harder.

Being a parent is something I want to do. Ever since I can remember, like most people, I've always wanted kids. I'll have to face the struggle of pregnancy, like most women do. But it's even more of a struggle when you're a woman with a disability. I don't know this for certain as I've never been pregnant, but doctors have told me about it, so I can imagine what it would be like.

Having problems with balance, a bad posture and struggling to walk is hard enough, but add extra weight to that, and I can imagine it's even harder. So I don't know how I would cope with having kids, but I know it will be a struggle if I do get pregnant. But it's not just having kids that will be a struggle if I decide to do this. There's more.

Living independently will be one of my hardest struggles. I'll have to face living independently without my parents and potentially on my own. I've always lived with people all my life as I'm only in my late teens now, and I've always relied on people to help with certain jobs that I can't do around the house. So, when I move away from home, potentially not having people living with me will be hard at first, as there won't be someone around on whom I can rely.

I will have to do everything for myself. I'm fine with that. I'm fine with living independently. But I'm not fine with disability getting in the way of what I'd like to be a fully independent life. That's when I'll have to swallow my pride a bit because I know it will get in the way of me living on my own.

But to stop this from happening so often, while I'm still living with my family, I'll have to practise normal activities that are essential but which I can't do very well at the moment, such as cooking (being one of the activities). Then, when I do move out and have to cook for myself, it won't be as much of a struggle and will be a bit easier to do as I'll have practised. But if this doesn't work, I'll have to think about other support networks.

I need to prepare for living on my own because I don't really want to rely on support networks, such as having a buddy, when others don't have to do that and don't have to prepare as much as I do. These are people who can move into a house and live in it as it is, without making any adaptations to make it more accessible and easier to get around when doing certain jobs: they can be sure of success and achieving new things.

I know that everywhere I go in life, whatever I do, whatever I achieve, there will be a struggle around every corner. There will be times when I'll be angry at life because of this and I'll want to give up. But it doesn't matter how many struggles I face; I will never give up. As I've said before, giving up isn't an option, and no matter how hard life gets, I must keep going and won't allow my struggles to defeat me or bring me down. I'm determined to do exactly that. When I move house, I may find one I really like and it might be my dream home but if it's not really accessible for me, I probably won't be able to buy it, and I must be prepared for that.

I'll always have to consider my limits and potential struggles as I go through life. Sometimes I'll have to adjust things around my disability and around what I'm doing. It will be even harder when, potentially, I've got no one there to help me; but to achieve the life I want, I'll happily go through any kind of struggle to get to where I want to be in life.

Chapter Nineteen

Low Expectations

"There's a very high chance that she'll never walk or talk, and she may be wheelchair-bound for the rest of her life."

The statement above is very similar to the words used by the doctors to inform my mum and dad after I had been diagnosed with cerebral palsy at just over one year of age. Sixteen years on, I am proud to be able to say that I can walk and talk and have hardly used a wheelchair in my life. For a long time, that feeling of being proud of myself has stayed with me. In my head, I've proved the doctors wrong and so, at times, I have felt the need to show off a bit, to be honest with you, saying, "Look at me now, doctors". However, over time, I have experienced the feeling of wanting to show off about proving the doctors wrong less often, and don't want to make this point as much as I used to. There are many reasons for this.

I don't want people who have the same disability as me, but more severely, feel they need to be like me but have failed because they're not as able-bodied as I am. I've had this feeling on many occasions. On top of this, I don't want to feel triumphant that I proved the doctors wrong for being able to do the stuff they said I wouldn't be able to do because, even though that's a good thing, I'm still disabled and that's really hard. Most importantly, though, I was very young when my parents were given the diagnosis and as time has passed I have come to realise that, in a way, I was a write-off from a very young age. It's as if the doctors gave up on me just because I have a disability.

I feel as though, when anyone is first diagnosed with a disability, everyone else expects them to be useless and to just sit in the corner watching people around them get on with their lives. Many of those diagnosed with disabilities such as cerebral palsy are probably told what I was told when I was first diagnosed, which I find unfair in many different ways. Yes, we may be disabled, but that doesn't mean we're useless in every way and can't do anything for ourselves.

This may be a bad example but let's say, if you were to break a window by accident and then hear that the window will never be fixable: it will stay broken forever, that's a bit like it was for me — and I'm sure for many other people across the world living with cerebral palsy — when we are first diagnosed with it.

We were the broken window that could never be fixed. But that's not true, because there is nothing broken about us at all. Yes, we may have cerebral palsy or another disability, but we're not broken, and we definitely don't need to be fixed in any way. I think the bleak comments that were made when I was first diagnosed portrayed my disability as a totally negative condition, which was being assessed before I even had the chance to live life. I was just one year old, and you could say I was already expected to be a "vegetable".

Over time, I have wondered: what if the doctors hadn't talked about the things that I wouldn't be able to do, and instead, had given my parents a bit of hope and said something along the lines of "There's a chance that she'll be able to walk and talk and do things for herself"? Maybe if they had had higher expectations of me, there would've been a lot more hope, which is what every parent needs when their child is diagnosed with a disability. Maybe, then, disability wouldn't be seen as such a negative issue and fewer people who have disabilities would be seen as useless and in need of being cared for.

I've not been expected to be able to do things all my life due to my disability, because people often think that, if you have a disability, you are automatically someone who needs care all the time. I've been told many things as a result of my disability: I've been told that I may never walk or talk, that I will never be able to swim, I will never be able to drive a car, I will never be able to make a drink for myself. Normally, this inspires me to prove to people that I can or will do these things, because they don't really know that I won't be able to drive a car or make a drink for myself. None of us knows whether any one of us will be able to do these things.

People have low expectations of those who are living with a disability and I know I am told these things because I'm disabled. They just presume that we'll never be able to do all sorts of things because we're less able-bodied than most people.

However, I've also been told these things by people who don't really know me that well; they include specialists I've seen because I'm disabled. This makes me angry at times because I've only met some of these specialists once or twice, or perhaps they've only met me on one occasion. Therefore, they can't know all about what I can do and can't do; they don't know how I go about doing things, what I struggle with and what I don't struggle with. But then, there's my disability; so, even though they don't really know me physically and don't understand my abilities, because I'm disabled, they expect so little of me. This is no doubt based on the assessments they've undertaken with me to test my physical abilities, which you could say is fair enough.

But here's the thing — some days I'm more tired than others and can't do things that I might have been able to do the day before. And so, if I have a physical assessment with a specialist on a day when I'm quite tired, then obviously the assessment is going to show the worst of my physical abilities. The specialist is then, of course, going to observe that I can't do some things, when actually I can; it's just that, on the day I see the specialist, I can't do these things because of my tiredness. I guess that's part of the reason why I've always hated the specialist assessments I have to undergo.

Being told that I can't do certain things hits me quite hard and makes me feel quite sad. It's as if I'm being told that I'm useless and lazy or I'm not trying hard enough to do what others can do. But I don't want to feel I'm lazy or useless, because that's a pretty crap feeling to have. Sometimes, when you're told you can't do something because you have a disability, you feel a whole range of negative emotions towards yourself and the world in general, just because people have low expectations of you.

It's as though you're judging yourself based on what people's expectations of you are. That shouldn't happen at all, and people shouldn't judge others based solely on what they see, not really knowing them that well or, in some cases, at all. Just like the saying "Don't judge a book by its cover" — read the book first before you judge it.

The specialists are often referred to as experts and so they're probably right when they tell me I can't do something, but in my eyes, they're not experts on my life and how I live with cerebral palsy. As I've already said, most of them don't know me well enough to be able to pronounce on what I can or can't do, so how can they be an expert if that's the case? Sure, they've probably seen many people like me, with the same disability as I have, but just because I have the same disability as someone else, doesn't mean I'm exactly the same as the other person and have the same abilities as they have.

Everyone's different: you can't say that one person will be unable to do a certain thing because another person can't do it; we're all unique and have unique abilities. I think the only expert in such situations is me. I know every single thing about my physical abilities and that's because I've lived with cerebral palsy all my life. I know what I can or can't do, I know that I may struggle with some things, I know how my body works and only I know that because I live in it every single day. So, to be told by someone that I won't be able to do something is quite annoying because they don't actually know me physically — no one does. How can they just presume that I won't be able to do something when that may not be the case at all?

It's not just the specialists that tell me what I can't do; it can be other people, who aren't 'experts' at all, but who just presume I can't do something other people can do because I am differently abled, which is sometimes the case but not all the time.

At school, we went on this trip to a woodland activity centre where there were all sorts of outdoor activities, from building a raft to climbing a wall. There was one activity which involved climbing, and deep down, I knew this was going to be harder for me to do, but I was willing to give it a go, as I did with most things. However, before I even had the chance to try this activity, my teacher or one of the instructors — I can't remember who — came over and told me I couldn't join in and do this activity. So, I asked why not.

They said that I would not be able to do it as it would have been too challenging for me. I had never undertaken an activity like this previously but already, before I had even given it a try, I was being told that I couldn't do it as it was too challenging for me. Now, I know this was meant in my best interests, but at the same time, it was a presumption on their behalf. Yes, it would have been challenging but I could still have given it a go — which is what I wanted to do. This occurrence was mainly down to people's expectations of me. They didn't expect me to do it, so they didn't even let me have a go at it which, in my eyes, is probably what they should've done. It is not the only time that something like this has happened.

I've been told that I can't join in with others simply because I'm disabled. This always happens because people expect so little of me and they don't give me the chance to exceed their expectations and prove to people that I can do things. It is often presumed that, because my body isn't fully able like everyone else's, I can't do anything that a fully able-bodied person can do. This isn't the case at all, and again, going back to the view that disabled people are "vegetables", people automatically presume that we can't do anything without even asking about our limits and what we can or can't do.

I've never had a say in situations where I've not been allowed to do something because of people's presumptions and low expectations, and so it feels as though I'm pushed to the side a lot of the time and my abilities are being overlooked. In the past, when there's been an activity I may have found harder to achieve, it would've been nice if someone had actually asked me if I wanted to join in and try it. But people's expectations come before that and so, at various times, I haven't been able to decide things for myself and find out whether I'd be able to try something new.

I find it very frustrating when people decide on my behalf whether I can do something or not, because I'm the only one who knows my own limits. So, surely, I should be the one deciding what I do and whether I can join in or not? I've been expected not to be able to do stuff all my life, and when I do something I'm not expected to be able to do, I get called things like "You're an inspiration", which makes me feel good about myself as it's kindly meant. However, at the same time, I don't like being called that because, in my eyes, I'm not an inspiration at all; I'm just living my life, doing what I can do and what my body tells me and allows me to do. How is that inspirational?

Because I was expected to be in a wheelchair, but wasn't in practice, I guess people saw me as an inspiration, but then that's just the way disabled people are expected to be in the world — in a wheelchair. Maybe, if the expectations of disabled people were higher than they are, people wouldn't be so shocked when we do stuff that other people do as a matter of course. Just because we're disabled doesn't mean we sit in a wheelchair all the time doing nothing — for some of us, this isn't the case at all. We shouldn't be expected to be like that, sitting around doing nothing — in my eyes that's just a stereotypical image of a disabled person. Yes, we're disabled, but we are also capable of doing all kinds of things, so we're just like others in this respect. Low expectations shouldn't get in the way of that.

Chapter Twenty

What School Life was Like for a Disabled Girl

Starting school is a massive milestone for every kid as they move into a new environment. For me, it was an even bigger one as I wasn't like most kids. At some point in my early life, the idea of me even being able to put on a school uniform was near to impossible, so it was a big thing for my family as well. They had watched me struggle more than most kids of my age, and you could say, witnessed one of my very first achievements.

They say "School days are the best days of your life", but they don't talk about the hard times that are part of those days. For me, my school days were both the best and the worst days. When I first started primary school, I wasn't seen as normal by all the other kids around me, and so they wouldn't treat me in the way they treated normal kids. Probably because I was seen as abnormal, it was a struggle for me to make real friends.

School life was a bit different for me. For a start, I couldn't write before the age of six like all the other kids did, which meant I couldn't take part in the same activities as they did in lessons, and which also meant I had to have a TA (teaching assistant) scribe for me. I also used to have to participate in speech, language and physio sessions in school time from the age of five, so I had to go out of class a lot.

At first, this wasn't bad, in my mind it was actually quite fun missing out on lessons and all the boring stuff you had to learn in class, instead doing physio exercises and learning more sounds and how to say words. When people saw me leave the room as I was going to these sessions, I didn't take any notice of them staring at me. But then, after a while, I got fed up with people coming to see me and taking me out of lessons to work on my speech and mobility over the years. When I was little, I used to wonder why so many people wanted to see me so often and why I was being taken away from joining in with what my classmates were doing and why I couldn't stay with them instead.

I was very popular with all these therapists coming in to see me, but in my class, I wasn't very "popular" at all and was mostly "the unpopular one" with very few friends. This would make me dread playtimes and lunchtimes because everyone had someone to sit and eat their lunch with and play with, but I didn't have that. I had to ask the other kids if I could go and sit with them and play with them. Every lunchtime it was a nerve-racking task because I knew that, if I did ask a group of kids whether I could sit with them, the chances were that I would either be rejected and laughed at, or they would allow me to sit with them but would never talk to me and would act awkwardly around me, or not even acknowledge that I was there.

I would have preferred to sit in a lesson where I didn't have to talk to anyone, rather than go and play with my classmates, because I had no one to play with most of the time. This made it very lonely for me as everyone had someone, but I had no one. What made it worse was that I'd also hear nasty comments made about my disability behind my back or even to my face, which lowered my self-esteem as I believed that these comments were true. Because of this, I didn't feel very confident at school at various times, because the comments I received made me feel horrible about myself.

I guess that the mean comments were the reason why making friends was even more of a struggle for me, as everyone would hear them and believe they were true. But then, I guess everyone was also scared of me because, back then, they had probably never seen someone with a disability before. Don't get me wrong, I had some good times at primary school as well, but it was very lonely for me most of the time, not just because I was bullied and struggled to make friends, but also because for most of my primary school life I was the only one with a disability. In a way it made me feel I was weird and as though I didn't belong in that school or in any school and I felt I stood out as an outsider.

But I didn't want to stand out. I wanted to blend in with the rest of my year group and the rest of the school. This was difficult because one of the things that made me stand out was the equipment I used around the school and in the classroom, which was noticed by others. The equipment I used included a special chair, a laptop, and a writing slope; when I had school dinners I had to sit on another special chair and use cutlery that was different from the cutlery everyone else used.

Obviously, when I used the equipment, this made me stand out even more, so I hated the equipment and sometimes I would ask the teachers and TAs if I might stop using it and instead use the equipment everyone else was using. But this wasn't permitted because I would struggle using the same equipment as everyone else, and the standard equipment wouldn't be suitable for me or fit my needs.

Deep down, I knew they were right, even though I didn't want to believe them and wanted to be like everyone else: my equipment was there to help me and even though it didn't make me look cool, I needed all of it. In a way, it was another barrier that was stopping me from being a normal kid. However, as rubbish as that was, the equipment helped me a lot in my school life, even though I hated it. As I came to the end of primary school, I was hoping that the equipment would go away and I could be like everyone else at secondary school. But I needed more transition days than the rest of the kids in my class needed before going to secondary school. I realised this was because the secondary school teachers needed to figure out what needed to be put in place in order to help me around the school, and this included equipment which was very similar to the equipment I had used in primary school.

As I moved from primary school to secondary school, I became even more stubborn than I already was, and decided I didn't want help at all; I didn't want to use the equipment that was there for me; and I didn't want anything that would make me look more disabled than I already was. At first, to fit in with all the other kids, I would try to avoid using my equipment as much as I could so that I would 'blend in' with the class instead of standing out as I had done in primary school. In my head, I thought that, if I did this, I would gain more friends because people wouldn't recognise that I had a disability.

But that wasn't the case at all. Not using my equipment didn't automatically mean I gained loads of new friends and it didn't hide my disability either because my disability is a physical one, which meant people still noticed it. So I just had to accept that my disability was noticeable and that it didn't matter whether I used my equipment or not, people would already know that I had a disability.

As time went on and I got older, I finally started to realise that the equipment wasn't there to make me look more disabled than I already was; the equipment was there to help me. As the workload increased, it dawned on me that using a laptop was easier than writing; I got tired less and could keep up with the work; and my chair was there to keep my spine straighter than it was so that my posture wouldn't deteriorate. Soon after I realised all this, I didn't care what anyone thought of me or my equipment.

Most of the time, people supported me and I was treated like everyone else, which made me feel good about myself and that I was part of the school. This was something that, as I've said before, I never really felt in primary school. But then there were other times when someone at school would call me nasty names; most of the time, those names were linked to my disability, as that was so obvious and people would see how I was when they looked at me and then be horrible about it. The names I was called were mostly "retard", "spastic" or "discombobulated". Sometimes, I would try to ignore them if they were said behind my back, but most of the time, they would upset me.

It didn't upset me because that person was being mean about me; it upset me because it made me feel that having a disability was a bad thing and that I was weird. It also upset me because it would bring to mind the bullying that I suffered in primary school and made me wonder whether I was ever going to be free from being put down because I was disabled.

Sometimes, I would cry about it and feel sorry for myself when I got home from school, and then there were other times when I would only be a little bit annoyed. Either way, I always picked myself up and carried on because, as harsh as it sounds, I was used to being called every name under the sun because of my disability. I had to recognise that there were always going to be people who would call me names and try to bring me down.

That's the reality — there are always going to be people like that, not just in school, but in the outside world as well. But sometimes when I was called names at school, I wondered whether I was seen in this way by everyone around the school, just because one person wanted to be cruel about me and my disability. That's when I would get upset and hate my disability even more than I already did. But then I learnt to ignore the people who tried to bring me down and just focus on what I needed to focus on. I knew I had family and good friends who supported me when situations like this occurred, which also helped me block out all the negative comments.

By the time I was approaching the end of my school life, I felt like a normal person and part of the school. I didn't feel that I was different to everyone else and had confidence that I was accepted by my peers. I was also studying for my GCSEs, but the way in which I sat for my mock exams was a bit different to the way the rest of the year sat for their mock exams. Whilst everyone else sat in an exam hall and wrote using a pen, I had to take my exams in a separate room with a TA sitting beside me in case I needed a scribe (someone to write the exam answers for me). Writing the answers myself would be a struggle for me and if I didn't have a scribe to write the answers, I could use a laptop instead.

That's what I eventually did to complete my mocks, but when I first started doing mock exams, I didn't want to use a scribe or a laptop and — yet again — was stubborn because I wanted to be like everyone else and write the exam answers myself. But when my teachers were marking the exam papers they realised that, the more I hand-wrote, the more likely I was to lose marks; my work would have been downgraded because the examiner wouldn't have been able to read my answers due to my handwriting not being as clear as other people's. So, because I wanted to do my best in my GCSEs, I swallowed my pride and started preparing to use a scribe in class so that I could get used to having one in the actual exams.

Unfortunately, due to the global pandemic caused by the Coronavirus, I couldn't actually sit my exams and had to leave school earlier than I should have done. Before I left school, I couldn't wait to leave, and was looking forward to no longer being a schoolgirl and going out into the world where I could be me and not have to pretend to be someone else to gain approval, as had been the case at school. But after I left, I realised how much I really missed school and sensed that I was going into an adult world where I would still have to face challenges. Even though I still miss school a bit, I have changed two things about myself that I didn't really attempt to do anything about at school. Those changes are, firstly, to be myself and not hide my disability simply to gain the approval of others, no matter where I am or who I'm with; and secondly, to accept help when needed. These two things are very important to me nowadays and they always will be. I think my experiences at school helped me to realise that.

Chapter Twenty-one

Making Friends

In life, we meet people from all kinds of backgrounds and sometimes, as we go through life, some of those people become our friends or even our best friends. For me, it doesn't work like that. I don't just meet someone my age for the first time and then we become friends automatically — which is how it works for most people of my age. I go through life like all of us do, but making friends is a little bit harder for me. And you've probably guessed it already, struggling to make friends is down to my disability, like everything else.

When people meet me for the first time, they don't see *me*; they don't take in my personality or what I'm like as a person. You see, when people meet me for the first time, they only see my disability, which makes them realise that I'm very different to them. This can put them off wanting to be friends with me and getting to know me as a person because the harsh reality is (and I've probably said this before a few times) that people don't like "different", which is tough for me because I *am* different.

I've met many people who are around my age and some of them do speak to me when we meet and are nice and friendly. However, most people don't acknowledge that I'm even present — they don't come up and ask to hang out with me or be friends with me. What this means is that, when I meet new people in social situations, it's down to me to make the effort and get talking to people and hope they will be friends with me eventually.

But it's not that simple. Just because I go up to someone and ask if I can hang out with them or talk to them, it doesn't automatically mean they are my friends. Most of the time, there's a kind of awkwardness in the air every time I've gone up to an individual or a group and asked the question, "Can I hang out with you?". This is all down to them getting used to the idea of actually being around a disabled person and probably trying to figure out how they can communicate with me. I fully understand that, whilst they're processing all this, it may be awkward for them to get to know me. At other times, it may be down to people being absolute idiots (in my view) and not wanting to give me the time of day, because being friends with someone who is "different" is probably "uncool".

This is hard, especially when it's something you can't change, so that making friends could become a lot simpler. Sometimes, I wonder whether, if I didn't have a disability, people of my age would see me for who I am and would want to be friends with me. As much as I hate to admit it, if I had no disability, this would probably be true. If I weren't disabled, making friends would be easier for me. Unfortunately I can't change that. I can't just randomly remove my disability, so that I'm not disabled any more. It doesn't work like that. But I've figured out that I shouldn't need to change myself to get people to think I'm cool and become friends with me — which is sadly what I have done in the past in an effort to make friends.

In a world where there are a lot of differences, people should be able to see past my disability; they should want to befriend me for who I am and accept me as a person. Unfortunately, my experiences of meeting people and trying to socialise and make friends with them show that it doesn't always work like that; people can't seem to get over the fact that I'm disabled in order to see me for who I am.

It sometimes makes me wonder if I have a meaning or if I'm worthless, and it also makes me wonder how people *do* see me. Do they see me as a real person? Does my disability make them think I'm different and not human? At times, I get angry about this, because we should be treating one another equally and not avoiding those who are a little bit different to everyone else.

At the same time, I've come to realise that people aren't necessarily avoiding getting to know and befriend me. They've probably never been near anyone who's got a disability before and need some time to get used to having someone like that around; they need time to break down the awkwardness I mentioned earlier. It's taken me a while to figure this out: in the past I thought people were being horrible and selfish by being afraid of befriending someone with a disability.

Because of this, sometimes I feel the need to prove to my peers that, just because I've got a disability, it doesn't mean I'm a weirdo or something and that I can do everything they can do. But I shouldn't need to get the approval of others for being good enough to be their friend. It shouldn't be like that; it shouldn't be necessary for me to feel as though I need to be approved of at all.

As sad as it sounds, I guess the truth is that, through my life to date, I've felt that I need to prove I'm just like others, despite my disability, in order to make friends with people. It has made me wonder what my worth is at times, because I've felt I needed approval based on whether I'm worth anything to anyone, or whether I'm a disabled girl who has no worth and is a person no one would even consider befriending.

At times, my apparent lack of worth has made me wonder if people actually see me or rate me as a person or if I'm just invisible to them, in the same way that my disability has made me invisible to others. In truth, I'm sick and tired of the fact that it's always me who makes the effort to gain friends, whereas there doesn't seem to be any effort coming from other people in my direction.

As tough as it is for me, I have to accept it's probably going to be like that for the rest of my life. But there's no point in letting that get me down by questioning my worth. I know I'm worth a lot more than certain people of my age who put off being friends with me because of my disability, because there are so many other people who do care about me and want to be friends with me; there are also more people out there whom I haven't met yet and who will want to befriend me in the future. And that's what I choose to think about — the people for whom I'm worth a lot, rather than the people for whom I'm worth nothing at all.

In the past, I've felt I had to change myself and my personality in order to be accepted by people who didn't know me or anything about me, but nowadays I refuse to change myself or my personality so that I can make friends. Real friends will accept me for who I am and not for what I could be, and I'm happy to have found them and will find more in the future. It's taken me a while to make real friends, but now that I've found them, I appreciate them. I appreciate them because I know it must have been hard for them to accept me at first, get used to my disability and adapt to being friends with someone who has a disability and isn't quite used to them. Despite all this, they've stayed by my side and stuck by me through thick and thin.

It's taken me a while to realise that, even though most of my peers will be put off being friends with me because of my disability, there are other people out there who are my real friends and won't see my disability or let it put them off getting to know me. They will see me for who I am, they will love me for who I am and want to be my friends.

However, as I can be quite negative at times, I sometimes forget this and focus on the people who don't want to be friends with me, because it makes me feel I need to fix myself a bit, whether it's changing what I wear or how I act. Again, I know I shouldn't do that or focus on the negatives, but as someone who's often been put down for having a disability, I've occasionally felt that, by having more friends, I will feel less badly about myself and believe there's nothing wrong with me — and that's why people want to be friends with me.

On the other hand, I don't want friends so that I can feel better about myself; in my view, that's not what friends should be for. I want friends who will keep me company and go shopping with me, but as I haven't got many friends, it can be really lonely at times, especially when my friends are busy and have other plans. When this is the case, I have no one to hang out with and I can't go shopping and do what others of my age do with their friends. I'm not like other girls of my age. I don't have loads of friends calling me up and asking me to hang out with them. That can be mentally and emotionally draining sometimes, when you look on social media and see people going out with their friends, you feel left out and that you're missing out on things you should be doing.

It's harder for me to do some things, such as going on a girly day out shopping, due to me not having many friends. It may be easy for others, but for me it can be quite difficult at times to achieve simple tasks such as going out shopping or other common activities. Sometimes I feel as though I'm not a teenager because I don't do these things as often as others of my age do, and it makes me feel as though I've been robbed of doing all this stuff.

But when I do meet up with my friends and we go out and do the usual stuff that teenagers do, all the loneliness and worries about missing out because I'm not good enough go away. I feel like a normal teenager again who's doing stuff and getting out and who's not stuck inside all day dwelling on the fact that I'm not going out as often as my siblings do. When I'm spending time with people who care about me and want me around them, that makes every negative feeling about not being wanted as a friend go away.

Over the years of being lonely and trying to make friends with people who quite clearly don't want to be friends with me and don't value me as a person, I have realised I'm worth a lot more than being that someone who is left out of things and who isn't accepted because they have a disability. My real friends are the ones I choose to focus on now and they are the ones I choose to spend time with, rather than with people who can't accept me for who I am. Over the years, I have learnt that your real friends will be by your side through thick and thin, whilst others will walk away when things get too difficult for them to handle.

Chapter Twenty-two

Learning to Know My Limits

1 used to think I was invincible, that I could do anything and everything, and that nothing could get in the way of me doing whatever I liked. I guess I still do think this at times, to be honest with you. But the truth is that I'm not invincible, especially living with a disability, which means you can't do anything and everything. There's always something that I can't do, that I will struggle to do, and that something is always going to be there.

A big part of accepting my disability was recognising that I have limits other people may not have and knowing what those limits are, so that I could get on with my daily life and not get tired out whilst doing so. As an observer, I've seen people undertake all kinds of activities in their daily lives — go to the shops, take the dogs out, meet up with friends, do household chores; these tasks amount to a ritual of activities that people who aren't disabled carry out every day — at least I presume they do. As a disabled person, I know I couldn't do half the jobs I've listed in a single day, as it would be too tiring for me. I would only be able to undertake a couple of the activities and I'd be tired just as a result of doing them.

You see, the thing is that I feel determined to carry out these activities, all of them within a day, even though I wouldn't be able to do them physically because of the strain they would cause. But I tend to overlook the physical strain. I'm going to be honest with you now and say that I don't know my limits. That's the confusing part — I'm writing about my limits, when actually I don't know them at all. I've always pushed myself to do stuff that I don't have the energy to do, and I'm too tired to do some things but do them anyway: I really push myself to do these things.

This is all down to my stubbornness. Because I'm so stubborn, I don't always know when not to do something, either because I'm already really tired at that point in time or it's too difficult for me to do, so quite often I experience physical strain. I don't know when to stop doing stuff and have a break in order to rest my muscles.

I've always been the kind of person who doesn't want to have a rest day, even though my body needs it, because I've always felt this pressure to prove to people that I'm not lazy and I'm willing to do anything and everything to show them that I may be disabled but I'm also independent. I guess laziness and independence are two big issues for me. Because I can walk and talk, I feel as though I need to carry on, not stop for a break and be as independent as possible. To me, stopping for a break from the things I do on a daily basis so that my body doesn't suffer too much strain, I see as laziness, and so I'm being lazy if I simply take a break and don't do stuff for a day or two.

Because disabled people can be seen as quite lazy by others, even though we're not lazy at all, I feel the need to break down the stigma attaching to disabled people which means they are seen that way; I want to prove to people that this isn't the case. I guess I've always felt the same about breaking down the stigma of how we may be seen by society so, because of this, I've put society and its views first, above my physical needs. I've always been worried about what people think of me — it's one of my weaknesses, to be honest with you, and I hate the thought that taking a break in order to rest and avoid damaging my body can come across as lazy, when I'm not being lazy at all.

Deep down, I know people won't think this of me and they'll understand that I'm disabled, which means I am different, even if I don't want to admit it at times. I think the reason why I worry about what people think of me is down to the bullying that I endured in the past and all the nasty comments that were made about me and my disability. This was a long time ago, but somehow it has still managed to leave an impression on me and has caused me to harbour this worry for a long time, as I feel people will have the same views about me as the kids at school did. I know that this shouldn't be a worry and that I shouldn't let the past get in the way of my future; I should focus on myself and my needs. My main focus should be on trying to find out exactly what my limits are and when to give myself a break, without feeling guilty about it.

I've never once put my physical needs first and so, because of this, in the past I have experienced all sorts of aches and pains. I get aches and pains on a daily basis anyway, so when I get aches and pains caused by me overdoing things, it's even worse. For me, this is a wake-up call that I do need to rest as I've gone beyond my limits and pushed myself way too hard. But do I? Of course, I don't — most of the time I stupidly choose to ride roughshod over these aches and pains, thinking I'm some sort of invincible warrior, which I am certainly not.

I'm so stubborn that I think, no matter how ache-y I am or how tired I feel, I just won't rest as I'm a failure if I do this, not getting on with life like everyone else but sitting at home resting. Then I get reminded by my mum or someone else that I'm different. I'm not like everyone else. I have different limits or even more limits than everyone else has, and they're right — I *am* different, even though I still hate the fact at times, I am different. I realise I can't do all the things that everyone else can, but the problem is that I don't always want to think about that, and instead, want to prove to people that I can do everything they can, when the fact is that I can't.

Yes, I can do most things, but I have a disability which means that I can't do everything. I am limited by what I can physically do. I do struggle to process this at times when I'm keen to do things for myself and be independent. It's always been a hard pill to swallow, even though I accept it a lot more now than I did in the past. Because I do want to live independently, I don't like the fact that there are going to be limits that will get in the way of this.

The future worries me at times, as I don't know exactly what my limits are. I'm worried that, one day, I'll go beyond my limits by doing something that I can't do, want to do and think that I'll be able to do, and then something bad will happen with the result that I'll hurt myself. My stubbornness will end up by not benefitting me at all. It's really important to me to try and find out what my limits are as I live my daily life, but it's hard to do this after such a long time when I thought that I had no limits and could do everything and that my disability wouldn't get in the way of that.

Unfortunately, in the past, as a way of learning that this isn't true, I've hurt myself by doing something that I couldn't actually do but thought I could do. I remember trying to shave my legs with a razor on one occasion — before then, my mum or my sister shaved my legs. As I was becoming a teenager, I didn't want my mum or sister to shave my legs any more and so I started trying to convince my mum that I could do it myself and that I didn't need someone doing it for me. My mum didn't really want me to do it by myself because of the danger that I might cut myself with the razor.

However, after a while spent convincing her that I could shave my own legs, she let me try doing it myself. So, for the first time, I tried shaving my legs myself with a razor. I stroked my legs with the razor about once and then — guess what? — I cut myself. Of course, I did. I cut myself because I was trying to do something I couldn't actually do — shaving my legs with a razor. Do you know what? Mothers are always right about things like this! Beforehand, my mum had warned me I would end up cutting myself, but I chose to ignore her because I thought I could do anything, including shaving my legs — , but in reality, I couldn't.

Cutting my leg with a razor was a real shock for me, it showed me that I wasn't as invincible as I had thought I was and that I did have limitations. At the time, the shock of this realisation really felt like the end of the world. I didn't want to live a life full of limits — I still don't, to be honest with you — but at that point in time, when I didn't accept that I was disabled and certainly didn't accept that I had limits, I thought that living a life with limits wasn't really living a life at all. I hated my life because I wasn't like everyone else and couldn't do all the things they could do.

Nowadays, I still don't like being limited by what I can or can't do, but I have realised I can live a good life even within limits, and yes, I can't do everything, but at least I'm lucky enough to be able to do most things, which is better than nothing. I'm still trying to learn what my limits are, and along the way, I won't be so stubborn and won't push myself to do things that I can't do, but I'm willing to learn what they are so that I can make life easier for myself.

Chapter Twenty-three

Why Me?

I don't mind being disabled. To me, without it, I wouldn't be Issy. I wouldn't be the person I am today. Without it, as sad as it sounds, I probably would have taken life a lot more for granted. I would have treated life as a joke and not seen what my purpose is and has been. I wouldn't have met such great people — whom I have only met because of my disability. To this day, I probably wouldn't have done as well as I have done or achieved what I have achieved in my life so far. Yes, my disability isn't what I'm all about but at many points in my life it has served a purpose, and that means something to me. I guess, because of all this, in a way my disability is a blessing in disguise.

However, there's a question that I've asked myself continually through my life living with a disability. The question is, "Why me?". There are billions of people out there in the world living their lives, so why was I one of around eighteen million people who were picked to live with cerebral palsy? I don't want this question to seem so negative any more, as it has been for me for a very long time. In this book, I've written quite a lot about how it has taken me a while to accept myself and my disability; about how, in the past, I hated myself for being disabled; and how I used to try hiding my disability to make it invisible to the world; and about all the negative emotions that I felt towards it and towards myself.

During those times when I used to see both myself and my disability as negative, I used to ask myself "Why me?" quite a lot, in a negative tone of voice. It was as though I was asking the universe why I had been picked to live such a purposeless, miserable life with a disability that I hated; every time I asked this, there would be no answer. But I wanted an answer, I wanted someone, or even something, to tell me why I was dealt a card such as this disability. I just didn't understand any of it. Had I done something wrong in my past life (if I ever had one) to deserve the pain of living with a disability? Why was I the one who had to be disabled?

I used to get angry that I never received a specific answer, and it would make me think the whole world was laughing at me, as if I was some sort of joke. That's why, whenever I asked the universe (or whatever higher being there is), "Why me?", I would never get a specific answer, because it was too busy laughing at me. It was as if I never deserved an answer. I felt I was being punished for something by having a disability, and all I wanted was an answer to why that was. But why didn't I get one? Why wasn't there an answer to the question of why I had to live with this terrible disability? I wanted to know why I had a disability and everyone else around me didn't. I guess I wanted an answer because I thought it would make me feel better about being disabled; in a way it would be like getting justice — the justice of knowing why I was disabled and had to struggle on a daily basis.

Because for a long time I didn't accept my disability, all I could see about being disabled were all the negatives around it, there was nothing positive about being disabled, and truthfully, I still don't think there is anything positive about the physical aspects. But I didn't see all the opportunities that lay in front of me. I didn't think that I could live a fulfilling life with a disability. Every time the question of "Why me?" came into my head, it was as though I was begging some higher being not to be disabled any more and to be free, free from the aches and pains that living with a disability brings, free from the social barriers that having a disability comes with, just free from being trapped in a body that I didn't want to be in any more.

That's what it was like. I felt trapped and imprisoned in my own body and so I desperately wanted to know what I had done to be trapped and restrained from living — that's how I saw it. There were many days and nights when I felt like this and simply didn't see the point of life. In my eyes, there was no answer to why I had a disability, and that's what most people (aside from the people who knew me best) saw in me, they just saw the disability every time they looked at me. So, surely my life was pointless because I was only seen as disabled and not for what I had to offer or for all the potential that lay in front of me? I felt as though part of me was invisible to the world.

But it wasn't pointless at all. I had so much potential ahead of me — even though I didn't see it and thought the world couldn't see it either, because of not knowing the reason behind my disability. I'm in a better place now, where I don't only see negatives all the time. I look at myself and have accepted aspects of my disability that I never thought I would accept back then.

However, there are still days when the question "Why me?" creeps up and takes my mind over. When this happens, it can be a bad day for me during which my disability gets on my nerves, whether it's because I've fallen over, or someone has commented on my disability, or any one of many other reasons. So, in these situations, I ask "Why me?" simply because I do want to know why I am disabled. I want my disability removed from me immediately and want to be 'normal' (whatever normal is), so that I don't fall over or won't have people making comments on my disability.

I still often think about why I was picked to live with a disability when the disability could have been given to someone else instead of me. It's unkind of me to think like this, I know, but in a situation where you're having a bad day, as I've mentioned, and you're desperate to be "normal", when in society you're not seen as "normal", you think about anything that will help, because you're in a negative mindset and feeling sorry for yourself. As I've come to accept my disability much more, I don't really ask why I'm disabled, as being disabled isn't really a massive problem any more — it's part of who I am. Sure, it's really hard on some days and they're the days when I do ask this question, but I can't change it — I can't take away my disability just like that. Also, I'm used to it by now, so I guess I've stopped asking because, even if I did get an answer, it wouldn't change anything.

It's about learning to live with being disabled, learning to accept it and not asking the "why" question as much; it won't benefit you and you would see your disability in such a negative light because you'd be questioning it all the time — which is what I was doing. However, the question "Why me?" doesn't always make me think about how unfair it is that I'm disabled and not many other people are, it also fascinates me in some ways too. As I see it, there will never be an answer to this question, apart from the scientific answer to how my disability developed from birth, but for me, and I'm sure for many people all over the world living with a disability, that's not the answer we want. I know for sure that the answers I want to the "why" question are: Why did it have to be me? Why was I picked to live with cerebral palsy? And why does it mean that I'm so different from others in this world in so many ways? These are the answers I want. I don't care about the scientific side of it — that side bores me. I simply want to know, "Why me?".

I like to think that this disability was bestowed on me for some purpose, perhaps because someone out there cherry-picked me to be disabled because they thought I'd be strong enough to handle it. This thought gives me comfort because, to me, it seems as though I was given this disability for a reason, that maybe my disability provides me with a mission to change people's views of it and to show them that *dis*ability doesn't mean *in*ability. By thinking in this way, it's better than getting an answer.

Over the years, I've learnt that I must be disabled for a reason, even though it isn't the best thing to have, there must surely be a reason why I am disabled. These days I don't necessarily need to know what that reason is any more whereas, before, I was desperate to find out why I was born with a disability. I have always believed that everything happens for a reason in this world; we may not know the reason, but that's the beauty of it. It's OK not to know the reason behind everything that happens in this world because, to me, that's what makes life so much more interesting. We don't need to know the reason behind everything that happens. We should just trust what life has in store for us and believe it will all work out in the end.

I will never know the reason why I am disabled because, more than likely, there isn't one and there doesn't have to be one. I appreciate that I was meant to be disabled, and because there's no reason behind it, I find it mysterious, in a good way, that this is the case. So that I can accept my disability, I also need to accept and understand that there will never be a reason why I am the way I am, apart from the scientific argument. When I finally realised that the question I had been asking for years and years doesn't have an answer and never will, it was like a fresh of breath air. It was as though it was meant to be. I was meant to be disabled for a reason that doesn't need an answer.

To you, my readers, this might sound completely crazy as you may be thinking that I shouldn't be disabled, I should be like other people of my age out there who have more physical freedom than I do, and that's probably one version of the truth, as my life would be much easier to live if this were the case. But it's not the case and so, because I think that everything happens for a reason, I also believe I am meant to be disabled and not like others which, you could say, is for a reason as well. It's taken me a while to try and understand why I am disabled, and I still don't fully understand why I am. Why me? I don't know. I will never know, but that's OK. I was put on this earth for a reason, my body picked me for a reason, and I may never know what that reason is, but that's OK. There doesn't have to be a reason or an answer for everything; life has a plan for us, and we should trust that plan.

Chapter Twenty-four

The Physical Side of Being Disabled

It's quite obvious that I have a physical disability as I've spoken about it many times already. I've also mentioned the words "physical" and "disability" many times and have placed them together many times as well. However, I've never actually told you how my disability affects me physically and what this can mean for me from time to time. It's kind of hard to explain to you guys what living with a disability feels like, as this is the only body I've ever lived in, but living in this body has made me something of an expert on how it does affect me physically. So that's my main aim here, to try to educate you guys on the physical side of what cerebral palsy is, and also explain how this can affect me and my lifestyle in many different ways.

If you were to see me in person, you would notice straightaway that my disability mainly affects the way I walk and talk, as I've mentioned previously. I normally walk with a limp because my right side is stronger than my weak left side, and so it's usually my left leg that causes me to limp. I don't feel this or notice it because it's normal to me — I don't notice anything odd about my walking as I'm used to the way I walk. If I were to look in a mirror as I was walking, however, I would notice how my way of walking is different from the way a person without a disability would walk. I would be able to pick up on the different aspects of how my cerebral palsy affects the way I walk, and my limp would just be one of these aspects.

I've always had a limp since I first started walking, it's always been a part of the way I walk and so, it's the norm for me. My walking has improved over time, though, and I guess that's down to the physio sessions I've participated in over the years, which have undoubtedly improved the way I walk. My walking used to be much worse in the past; I used to hold my hands up to my chest as my balance wasn't that good, so that, if I were to fall over, I'd be able to stop my head from hitting the ground by catching myself with my hands. I felt more stable walking with my hands like that and felt safer when I was walking. I also used to walk a lot more slowly than I do now and my limp was much more severe — I think that's why my walking was a lot slower. However, I've built up my strength over time by attending the physio sessions and learning different exercises that, in the long run, benefit the way I walk through gradual improvement and working on my balance and a whole load of other things as well.

As for the way I talk, this is another thing that's affected by my disability, as I've mentioned. To put it bluntly, you could say that I sound a bit drunk when I talk; that's not to say everyone else with cerebral palsy sounds like this when they talk, it's just how I sound, and it's the easiest way to describe it. Because of this, my speech isn't as clear as the speech of someone who doesn't have a disability. I never used to like the way I sounded when I spoke, and I still don't. Every time a video came on or some other recording of my voice, I would block my ears so that I didn't have to listen to the sound of it.

But I had to get over that because, even though I was having speech therapy sessions which did improve my voice and the way I spoke, my voice was always going to sound a bit drunk. So I forced myself to get used to listening to my own voice and not recoil every time I heard it, because I couldn't change my voice — all I could do was improve it.

My walking and talking are probably two of the biggest barriers that I face as someone living with a disability. They get in the way of things in my life, such as socialising with others, as people can't really understand what I'm saying. Some don't want to give me the time of day because they find the obvious barrier to getting to know me quite hard to break down and overcome. Joining in with certain activities, especially physical ones such as running, was a big issue for me at school. When sports days happened, in every running race that I took part in I would end up coming last, which would leave me disheartened as I was so fed up with coming last every time. Lots of things in my life are affected by the way I walk and talk and the barriers they have created over the years.

This is one kind of barrier where I would take absolute pleasure in kicking its (metaphorical) backside, as it's the biggest barrier in my eyes and prevents me from doing many things, such as the activities mentioned above and many others as well. It's very irritating, but that barrier will always be with me, whether I like it or not. I can't get rid of it because it's there due to my physical disability and how this affects me, so it's unlikely that it can be removed and I can't kick its backside, as much as I would like to.

However, what I can do and have been doing ever since I can remember is improving my mobility and my walking in general, and also improving my speech. I don't have physio or speech sessions any more, but when I did, I used to find them quite boring and would do anything to get out of them, as I thought they were absolutely pointless and didn't help me at all. But now, looking back, I have realised that, without having attended those physio sessions, my mobility wouldn't be as good as it is now, and if I hadn't attended the speech therapy sessions, my speech wouldn't be as clear as it is now.

I wouldn't have been able to do the things I've done without these speech and therapy sessions so, in the end, they've benefitted me quite a lot, even if I did find them boring and pointless at first. The barrier that remains because of my speech and mobility issues is a lot smaller than it could've been if I hadn't attended physio sessions or speech therapy.

I sometimes wish I didn't have to live with a physical disability so that I could just go out and live a life that's free from aches and pains and appointments and all the things that come with being disabled. I think it's normal to wish this, but at the same time, I'm glad I have a disability, as I now appreciate the sense of achievement that comes from being able to do the simplest things in life; walking and talking mean a lot more to me than they would've done if I didn't have a disability, because I've had to fight to achieve them.

The physical side of my disability has made me do a lot of fighting for a lot of things that I wasn't guaranteed at birth. On occasion, it's been great, appreciating the little things a lot more and taking life a lot less for granted than I might've done without a disability, but at the same time, the physical side of my disability can be utterly crap as well.

As I've stated many times before, having a physical disability and being physically disabled means being restricted and not being able to do all the things that your siblings or friends might be able to do. I hate the fact that I may never be able to have children of my own because it would be too physically demanding for me; I hate the fact that I may need to use a wheelchair one day as my disability might mean my physical health will decline; I hate the fact that I'm not as physically able as my family and can't do things they can do and will continue to do in the future.

This is all part of the crap that comes with being disabled. It's not always about the scientific side of it and how some people view cerebral palsy and it's not simply how it affects an individual living with it: sometimes the physical side of being disabled can be more than just the physical side and how it affects you. This side can also be tiring, frustrating, mentally draining at times. It can be a whole range of things, and it's more than just having a limp when you walk or having speech that's unclear. I guess there are mental aspects that I have dealt with too, due to having a disability.

Of course, the physical side of it can be utterly crap, walking differently and talking differently, and then there are all the aches and pains that come after a day of doing physical activity which puts a strain on your muscles;, but at the same time, it can be really fun as well.

Now, in the past, I have been a bit naughty and played the disabled card a few times to try and get out of stuff. Stuff being, not having to wait in the queue for a ride at a theme park, as I get to skip the queue due to my disability. This is absolutely awesome. Less time in queues, more time on rides — what more could you want? This isn't really playing the disabled card, as I do have a disability and have the right to skip the queue; but the thing is, I could queue in line even though it might be a bit painful for my muscles, but I choose not to. Obviously, if I had to queue I would, as my cerebral palsy isn't as bad as it could be and it wouldn't be that much of a big deal if I had to queue, but I'd rather skip it, just as anyone else would.

I have played the disabled card for a few other reasons besides being able to skip the queue for a ride, which is just one example. Having said this, sometimes I really do have to play the disabled card because something may be too hard for me to do. In these cases, the disabled card is needed, but at other times, it's not needed as much but I use it anyway, as it does help me get things done more quickly and have more fun, or I might use it for other reasons.

What's also good about being disabled is using a wheelchair in a way that's fun. Now, normally I hate using a wheelchair, but sometimes it can be really fun. When I first got a wheelchair, I used to scoot myself across the garden as fast as I could, which was epic. What's not fun about scooting really fast across the garden in a wheelchair? I can also be lazy at times and get out of walking so that my wheelchair acts as my legs, and I don't have to walk around everywhere like everyone else. I see this as some kind of privilege, as my legs won't ache and I simply don't have to walk, especially if it's muddy; a wheelchair becomes my best friend then, as my trainers won't get muddy. Bonus! I'm sure loads of people would rather be in a wheelchair than have to walk in muddy conditions.

So, there are loads of fun times as well as loads of crap times that come with having a disability. In my case, the fun times might be fun for the wrong reasons to some people, such as using the disabled card on occasions when others may not use it. But for me, these fun times get me through the days of living with a disability, as they make me think that not all of having a physical disability is hard and that there can be positives too, which make living with a disability sort of worthwhile.

The physical side of my disability has been one of the biggest battles that I've had to deal with every day, to be able to live the life that I wish to live, the life I dream of living, but I think I'm doing all right with this battle. It's been hard, but I've been able to fight my way through it so far, and that's what I'm going to continue to do, so that my life isn't controlled by the physical side of my disability and I can live life as fully as I possibly can.

Chapter Twenty-five

Achievements

Life is too short. That's what I tell myself every day when I wake up in the morning. I didn't actually realise this until now. That's why I want to achieve as much as I possibly can in this short but fantastic life. I live every day just as I've been living them over the years. I've achieved a lot in my lifetime so far, from learning to walk and talk to riding a horse. These are things that I never thought I'd be able to do. I don't really talk about them much because it feels as though I'm blowing my own trumpet, but I'm going to right now.

My first-ever achievement was learning the basics of walking and talking. When I was around the age of two, the doctors said this wouldn't be possible for me and that I would have to rely on a wheelchair to be my legs. But that wasn't the answer for me. I didn't want a wheelchair as my legs. I wanted my own legs to allow me to be like other kids, to walk and run and do whatever I wanted. So, from a very young age, I was going to physio appointments so that, eventually, I would be able to walk like everyone else and not sit in a wheelchair watching everybody else walk around and do stuff. Neither I nor my family wanted that.

So, after a few years of physio, when I was around four years old, I took my first-ever solo steps for the first time, without any aids supporting me. When I first did this and started walking on my own without any aids, most kids of my age were already running and doing all the usual stuff a four-year-old should be doing at that age. But even though learning to walk didn't happen at around one year old for me, as it did for everyone else, I managed to walk in the end, and yeah, it might have been a bit later than one year old, but at least I was walking — and for me that was a big achievement.

Walking meant that I became more independent and didn't have to use a wheelchair as well; if I hadn't learned to walk, I wouldn't have been able to do most of the things I've done in my life to date. Around the time I was learning to walk, I was also learning to talk as well. Before this, my main way of communicating with others was through sign language as I couldn't talk yet and so, in order to start talking like everyone else, speech therapy sessions became the way forward. In these sessions, I was mainly learning new sounds to begin with, and then transforming the sounds that I learnt into words.

They were simple words such as "mum" or "dad" or "banana", but it was another step forward in enabling me to communicate with everyone else more easily than in sign language — as not everyone knew what signing was or how to sign to communicate. After going to numerous speech therapy sessions during my early years, in the same way as I attended physio sessions, my speech started to progress and soon, I was learning even more new words and then, not long afterwards, I started to put those words into small sentences, such as "Drink, please" or "Can I have a banana?".

Even though they were small sentences, and my punctuation wasn't the best, over time my speech was improving more and more. People could understand what I was trying to say and therefore they could meet my needs, understand what I was trying to tell them as well, and also talk to me more. Learning to talk meant that I could do more by way of communicating with others, and even though my speech was unclear to most people, my family and those closest to me could understand me and what I was saying. Most of all, it meant that I had a voice for years to come, not only to talk to people but also to give my opinions and have a say in things that impact me in my life.

Being able to walk and talk are things that I will always be grateful about, for the rest of my life. Having the privilege of being able to do things that most people take for granted and don't even think about means everything to me. It has made me a lot more independent, and I've been able to take part in activities over the years that the doctors said would be impossible for me to do. I will appreciate having this privilege forever.

I've achieved other things too and one that I still love is horse riding. Horse riding has been in my family because my nan loved it and so, when I was around eight-years-old, she and my mum encouraged me to try out the hobby that my nan had enjoyed when she was young. So, that's what I did, I tried it out at a local RDA (Riding for the Disabled) centre. I remember the first time I got on a horse I loved it. I loved being high off the ground and being able to keep my balance to stay on the horse — I loved everything about it.

I went riding for two years at the same RDA centre, and during that time, I learnt how to trot, how to stir a horse and how to stand up in the saddle. Every time I went on a horse, I felt free from everything. I felt I could let go of my worries and negative feelings for once, and just concentrate on riding a horse and becoming good at it. As well as the achievement of being able to ride a horse, I also made a hobby out of it and shared that hobby with my nan. Because of this, my nan took me to the Paralympics in 2012 to see the equestrian events, which was great as we got to go to London and see the Paralympians live in the stadium. Horse riding was a hobby that bonded me and my nan together.

Horse riding brought so much joy to my life and still does to this day. But when I was ten-years-old, I stopped for a little while, so that I could focus on other things, such as school. During that time, my nan kept reminding me of how much she would love me to start horse riding again, and I actually missed going horse riding every week as well. So, when I was thirteen, I started doing it again.

This time, though, I didn't go to an RDA centre to ride. I went to a normal riding stable, since I was a little bit older and wanted to be a bit more independent when I rode a horse. It had been a while since I had ridden, so I was a bit nervous about what it would be like on my first day back riding, and not having the same support as I had enjoyed at the RDA, which was new to me. But as soon as I got on a horse again and started riding, all the feelings I experienced when I had first mounted a horse came back to me, and I immediately fell in love with horse riding all over again.

This time, though, it was even better as I was riding a horse on my own without any assistance next to me and so I loved it because I felt more independent than I did when I was riding at the RDA. I loved it as much as I did the first time that I had ridden a horse and it felt like it did when I first started riding. I don't go horse riding any more, but it will always be one of my favourite things to do.

Horse riding has been one of my biggest achievements and I developed a hobby out of it as well. And another big thing that I've achieved in my life, and am still achieving, is raising awareness of disabilities. Growing up with a disability and observing the negative attitudes that some people have towards people with disabilities has made me want to change people's views about disabled people so that, one day, people like me with a disability will be seen and treated just like everyone else.

So, to be able to do this and try to change the way that disabled people are seen in the world, I created a PowerPoint presentation that's about my life with cerebral palsy and everything that defines it. After I had completed the PowerPoint slides, I delivered a presentation to my class and showed them what I had done. They really enjoyed it and it helped them understand a bit more about me and my disability.

As well as showing it to my class, I entered a competition. This was a competition in which thousands of kids with all kinds of disabilities put up a presentation about living with a disability. Whoever won the competition got to produce a video for a website which educated people generally and teachers especially about disabilities and also win a hundred-pound book voucher for their school. And a few months after I had entered the competition, I found out I had won it, which meant that I got to do the video and also won the book voucher for the school.

This meant that, whilst the video was being filmed, I showed my presentation to the whole of my year group. I was pleased with this because it meant I was educating even more people about disabilities, so that they would get a better understanding about what disability is. I also held an interview with my mum in the video, which was mainly us talking about what it's like living with a disability or living with someone who has a disability. By now, the video has been seen by teachers all across the UK.

As well as making the video, I have also given a few talks to audiences, composed mainly of teachers and other people working with people who have disabilities, to try and educate them a bit more about disabilities. This is what I wanted to achieve when I was giving talks to all these teachers and specialists and I hope that, by giving the talks, I have raised awareness of disabilities so that people don't view disabled people negatively and have a better understanding of it. I've wanted this to happen for a long time now and I hope that, by giving these talks, I have made an impact and increased the likelihood of this happening.

These are just some of the many things that I've achieved in my life so far and every one of my achievements has meant something to me, whether it's learning a new skill or trying to make a difference in the world in some way. Everything that I achieve is cherished, as I never thought I'd be able to achieve the things that I've achieved so far. It makes me grateful that I have been able to do all this and I look forward to achieving new things every day.

Chapter Twenty-six

Going into Adulthood with a Disability

I've always worried about what life will be like for me when I become an adult, which is going to be quite soon actually. What will I have to face? Will I be able to do all the things that a typical adult is able to do? Will I be able to live the life that I want? At present, I don't know the answers to these things, and I don't know what will happen in my adult life. As a person who's always wanted to know what's happening on a daily basis and likes to plan things ahead, this is a new experience for me. I will never be able to plan my future or what happens in it and I think this scares me the most, not knowing what will happen because I don't have control over the future — I have to let life do that for me. There were many struggles which I had to face in childhood, and I'm worried about the struggles I'll have to face in adulthood. It's quite obvious that I'm not like any other kid and I'm different, so I know I'm not going to be like any other adult and will be different from most adults. I can't just turn eighteen-years-old and then automatically become an adult: life's not like that for me, it's not as easy as simply becoming an adult and getting on with things in the same way as other adults do.

For me, going into adulthood means doing a lot of planning, finding out what I'll need so that I can get on with daily life, continuing to break down the barriers that are likely to be present, wherever I go. All this is a bit overwhelming for me. I don't even know how to find out about all these things as I haven't had to do so in the past. It's always been my parents who have been there to find out what I need and sort out all this kind of stuff. If I'm honest, as I haven't had a normal childhood on a physical level, like my siblings and my peers, I don't expect to have a normal adulthood either.

I do sometimes wonder how adults manage adult things, and I'm not talking about paying bills or doing a whole load of housework; I'm talking about driving a car, going abroad on your own as some adults do, and working a 9-5 shift without getting so exhausted that you have to take a day off work because of it. How do they do it? I'm sure that, although most teens don't understand how to be an adult, it will come naturally to them as they won't have to worry about their physical health when entering the adult world — unless they have a disability.

However, for me, adulthood won't come as naturally as moving out of your family home, getting a job that's suitable for you, and living independently, just like that. I hope all these things will come naturally to me, but as I've said previously, in my life so far nothing has come naturally as it has done for others, so I don't have much faith that adulthood will come naturally to me either. I know there are going to be things that will be harder for me to do.

It would be great if I could go to university before I enter the world of work — and that's what I'm planning on doing as the next step, after I finish my college course. This is a dream that I would like to achieve and I look forward to doing so as well; but the dream of going to university will be a challenge for me whereas, for someone without cerebral palsy, going to university would be much easier to achieve. I may be completely wrong, but if a young person without a disability wants to go to university, what they probably have to do by way of preparing for this is to visit a few universities to see which ones they like, assess the area they're in, pick the university they like best, and then apply to go there. If they get in, they will obviously live there, with a bit of help to move in, before eventually getting into the university routine and making friends. They'll be living an independent life pretty much from then on. This is how I dream of university being for me, but even though it's probably the norm for most people going to university, it probably won't be the norm for me — if I do go to university.

For me, moving to university will probably be very different. Looking at universities is definitely something I want to do, not just because I need to go and see whether I like the university and the area it's in, but for other reasons as well. These other reasons include finding out whether the university is accessible, how big the building is and whether I'll be able to walk round it every day without getting tired. I need to view the area it's in, find out whether the paths in the city or town where the university is are accessible and whether I'll be able to walk down those paths without there being a high risk of falling over and hurting myself. This is a big worry as I don't really want to risk having an accident simply by walking down the street.

I need to find out whether I'll require extra support in the form of a carer who can come in and help me with things I struggle with, such as cooking, or I may need special equipment that can be installed at my university flat, so that I won't have difficulties living independently. In addition, I need to consider whether I want to go to a university far from home or close to home. If I were going to a university close to home, then my family would be nearer to me, so if something were to happen and I needed them, they wouldn't be that far away and would be able to get to me easily.

However, if I were to move farther from home, it would be harder for my family to come and see to me.

At the same time, however, part of me does want to move farther from home, to go and explore a different place and be in a completely different area from the one where I live now. But I know it would be a harder task, if I do move away from home to go to university, than if I were to stay much closer to home. There will need to be a lot of planning to prepare me for going to university anyway, so if I moved further away from home, even more planning would be needed.

Planning! I hate planning my life. Even though I'm scared about life taking control of my future, I would rather this happened than for me to plan my every move in life. You can't plan life — it's not a wedding or some kind of formal party, so why would I need to plan different stages, such as going to university? I'm being over-dramatic when I talk about needing to plan my every move, because that's not what I have to do at all, but that's what it feels like. Most people do have to plan for stuff, such as going to university or getting a job, but probably not to the extent that I'll need to. It's a question of how I'm going to do things that other people find simple to do, such as planning the equipment I'll need — this is what I'm going to have to think about, and certainly more than once in my adult life.

Most adults probably don't think about this stuff in their lives at all, as it doesn't involve things that are likely to happen in their lives — why would it? For me, considering things like special equipment, whether a job is suitable for me and my physical needs, and loads of other things besides, will become the norm for me in adult life. Of course, I would prefer not to have to consider all these things and would rather get on with being an adult without things like these getting in my way. Unfortunately, however, I can't change this. It's just something that I will have to put up with for the rest of my life.

At the same time, though, I would rather plan the kind of stuff that other adults may never have to think about, than not be able to live as independently as I have done to date and will continue to do, even if it means struggling more than I have in my life so far. I think I'm extremely lucky to be able to move into adulthood and have so many opportunities in front of me and so much life to live and dreams that I will hopefully achieve because, once upon a time, this was seen as almost impossible. I shouldn't complain about becoming an adult, as I am really lucky to be doing so in the first place, and there are so many people out there who have more severe disabilities than I do who will struggle more with adulthood than I will. I feel as though I don't have the right to complain. Yes, adulthood will be harder for me than it will be for most other people, but at the same time, I am still able to become an adult and do many things as an adult.

I know that going to university will involve much more planning before I can go there; I know that buying a flat or a house of my own will perhaps mean having to find accommodation that's been adapted to suit me and my needs; I know that being accepted for a job may be difficult; and that finding a suitable job in which my disability won't get in the way may be hard for me to find;, but at the same time, as much as I'm really worried about becoming an adult and all the things I've mentioned, and as much as it scares me, I'm also excited about it and look forward to achieving new things. The whole business of generally being an adult and seeing what's out there for me is thrilling.

It's been really hard for me to get to this point because all my worries have taken over for so long; I've only just started looking forward to adulthood and my future because I've learnt to focus on all the positives and not worry too much about it. I've got so much ahead of me and this outweighs all the worries I have about adulthood. Adulthood is going to be hard, but for every hard time that comes, there will also be fantastic times which will make adulthood worthwhile.

Chapter Twenty-seven

Hopes and Dreams for the Future

We all have dreams for the future, dreams that our lives will be full of happiness, and sometimes, we have a vision of what our lives are going to be like — I know I do anyway. Even though the future scares me at times, I look forward to growing up and fulfilling my hopes and dreams. It makes me determined to achieve as much as I can and do as much as I can, because life's too short to just sit around and do nothing.

Amongst my many dreams, there is one I hope to fulfil in the next few years, which is to go to university and study sociology. I have always loved the thought of moving away from home, going to university to get a degree and then finding a job that I really like. It has stayed with me from a very young age, and I hope that I'll be able to do this one day and start creating a life for myself. As much as I'm looking forward to this, it'll also be a huge step towards becoming independent as well, which is what I want. I will have to do stuff for myself at university as my family won't be there to do it for me.

Even though I look forward, hopefully, to going to university, at the same time it frightens me as I haven't been away from home before, and it will be hard for me as I can't do certain things myself. This will be tough because I'll be on my own when I'm at university and there will be a lot of stuff that I'll have to think about before I go there. This will include things like: How am I going to cook? How am I going to make friends and form a good social life? And how will I live independently? These thoughts cross my mind every time I think about going to university, as well as feeling excited, and nearer the time, I will have to think about how I'm going to do these things on my own.

Perhaps sooner than I think, I will have to consider these things in a bit more detail, including how I'm going to manage on my own and how I will do normal day-to-day things, without family or friends being around to help me. But even though it will be harder for me to be at university than it would be for a person with no disability, I'm determined not to let these fears get in my way. Going to university is something I want to do and I don't want to let my disability get in the way of it, because it's been one of my dreams for ages now. It's something that will be a struggle, for sure, but it's also a dream that I hope I'll fulfil some day in the future.

Another of my dreams is to meet someone, fall in love, get married and start a family. Ever since I can remember, I've always wanted to find someone who will love me for who I am and with whom, perhaps, I will have kids one day. I've always wanted this. For most people, this dream becomes a reality, but sometimes in my head I hear myself saying that the dream of having a family with someone may not become a reality for me as I hope it will. I tell myself this because, having reached the age of seventeen, I haven't really had a proper boyfriend so far, and when I think about boys or when I'm even near boys, it brings out the negative feelings I have towards my disability.

In a way, I feel as though, when boys look at me, all they see is this disabled girl who can't do anything and isn't the typical sort of girl boys usually want as a girlfriend or would even want to be seen with. So I ask myself why a boy would want a disabled girl as his wife if he doesn't even want her as a girlfriend? Sometimes, this takes away my hopes of one day finding someone with whom I can share my life; in all honesty, I don't think this will happen because boys see my disability before they see me.

For years, I was looking for a boyfriend because I was so desperate to experience what having a boyfriend and being in love would be like. I would ask myself whether virtually any boy I saw in the street or at school would make a good boyfriend, but every time I did that it just made me feel worse about myself, because I was sure that the boys I walked past in the street would not want me as their girlfriend. Over the years, my hopes of finding someone have decreased: I don't want to get my hopes up and then see them crushed because of not having a boyfriend in my teenage years. What made me feel even worse was that everyone else around me of my age had a boyfriend or girlfriend, so I don't look for a boyfriend any more or even want one at present. I'd rather focus on myself and getting what I want out of life.

If I ever did meet someone and it became a long-term thing, there would be a slight possibility that, one day, I might have kids with that person. Isn't that what normally happens when two people fall in love and get married — they have kids and start a family? For me, if I were ever to have kids, it would be great but also an extra struggle for my body to deal with, because of going through pregnancy. My body struggles on a daily basis in any case, and as I've said elsewhere, adding an extra load of weight wouldn't be helpful and would strain my body even more.

As much as it would be great to have a mini version of me running around, pregnancy would be hard. If I did decide to get pregnant then there would be loads of things I'd need to consider, such as: How am I going to get around everywhere with this extra weight pulling me down? How will I do things for myself? Will I need extra help? I don't know the answers to these questions and that's OK at present, as I'm not going to get pregnant any time soon while I'm still a teenager. But if the time ever comes when I do meet someone and want to have kids with them, these are amongst the many things I'll need to consider when trying for a family.

At the same time, I have a fear of not being able to get pregnant and have kids due to my disability getting in the way, and even though there are other ways of starting a family, as always, I want to be 'normal' and do things the way other people do them. I think about this a lot when I'm picturing my future life, and also wonder whether I'll get the life I want due to my disability getting in the way — and that worries me. But I've learnt to forget about worries and look forward to the future. Even though the thought of not meeting someone, falling in love, getting married and having kids worries me, at the same time I'm excited about the future and what it will have to offer. Even if I don't have kids or get married, there are other dreams ahead of me that I probably will be able to fulfil.

Going travelling and seeing the world is another dream — much easier than pregnancy — that I hope to fulfil in the future. I've always liked the thought of exploring other countries and seeing different cultures. I think I want to do this even more now that I know I could do it. I'm quite able-bodied despite having a disability and therefore, in my mind, I'm thinking: Why wouldn't I do it if I had the chance? But even though I'm reasonably able-bodied, I am not as able-bodied as someone who has no disability. If I do choose to go travelling, there are loads of things that I'll have to consider, such as: Will I need another person to go travelling with me? Will I become very tired from moving around a lot? Will I need to make adaptations when travelling to make it easier for myself? When I'm thinking about the future, it makes me angry at times, because I have a disability that holds me back from doing things and I'm not fully able-bodied like everyone else. Going travelling may not be as easy for me as it would be for people who don't live with a disability.

Before I do stuff like this, my disability has to be a priority; I wish it didn't need to be, because my priority should be fulfilling my dreams, no matter what, and even though it'll be hard at times, that's what I'm going to do. Although I will probably need to make adaptations before I go travelling, I'm determined to do it, no matter how many adaptations will be needed, so that I can travel and explore the world.

When I'm dreaming about what I want to do in the future, I sometimes forget to think about how I'll be able to achieve my dreams with a disability and whether I'll even be able to achieve them; so I don't really think about all this stuff. I'm not like other people and everything I do in life, such as travelling, needs to be thought about a lot. Sometimes I find this unfair, because I can't just randomly decide to go out into the big wide world one day and achieve what I want to achieve, hoping for the best like most people probably do. Everything I do has to be thought about and my disability has to be included in these thoughts. I have to think about stuff, such as, "What will I struggle with?" or, "What will I need in order to achieve things in my lifetime?".

However, with or without a disability, life's too short not to do what you want to do with it. Even if my disability gets in the way sometimes, I've learnt that it has to revolve around me and not the other way round. Don't get me wrong, in the future I may have to fulfil my dreams differently from how a person without a disability would, and that's OK if I want to live the life I'd like to live. I get it that sometimes I will have to do things differently, even if I don't want to, but it doesn't matter how long it's going to take to live the life I want to live, I'm still going to live it. In my eyes, you only get one life and that life is there for you to live as you choose, whether you have a disability or not. What I've learnt over the years is that having a disability doesn't have to control your life, your life is there for you to live as you wish.

Chapter Twenty-eight

You Don't Look Disabled

Sometimes, people get shocked about the way I look or what I wear or what my hobbies are. In the past, I didn't know why that was, as I am the person I am and know what I'm about. Then there have been other times when people have told me that I don't look disabled, or they don't even notice I have a disability because of the way I look.

A while back, I would've enjoyed being told this, as I didn't appreciate looking like a disabled person and so hearing stuff like this would have been music to my ears. Nowadays, being told this bothers me at times, and for a while, I couldn't put my finger on why it bothered me so much, but then I came to the realisation that it was because there is a stereotypical vision of how a disabled person should look. In society, this is a big issue. People often expect a disabled person to look a certain way or act in a particular way, and all those who have disabilities are expected to look exactly the same as one another. Because society has come up with a stereotypical vision of how a disabled person looks, when a disabled person doesn't resemble that stereotypical vision, it can often be a shock for people.

I know I am disabled; I also know that I'm a girl — a girl who likes makeup, a girl who likes to go out shopping, a girl who likes to walk the dog on her own, a girl who has similar interests and hobbies to those of other girls of her age. Most people don't really look into why I have the same hobbies as a non-disabled person and just see it as normal. However, there are often others who may question why I have the same hobbies as a "normal" teenage girl, and this is because I'm not the stereotypical disabled girl that some people expect me to be.

I have no idea what society's stereotypical disabled person looks like, I have no clue at all, but I can only imagine that it's someone who's very different from any other person of their age, looks-wise especially. I don't know why, at times, people ask me and others with disabilities why we don't look disabled. I don't know why this question even exists actually. Why does it exist? Why is it even a question? Why is it even asked? I just don't get any of this at all. Every time I hear this question, I think of many reasons why it might be asked, but I can't put my finger on just one specific reason, because I honestly don't know how a disabled person is expected to look. What's so shocking about me that makes my disability questionable? Is it because I sometimes wear makeup? Is it because I wear clothes that some may consider to be too trendy for a disabled person to wear? Is it because I do stuff that some may say I shouldn't be doing as a disabled person? Why is it that some people don't think I look disabled? How am I supposed to look in order to look disabled?

It's as though my disability is questionable; some people ask me this question when they aren't sure whether I'm disabled or not because, to them, I don't appear to be disabled because of how I look. It's as if I need to change myself or act in a certain way in order for society to register that I look disabled, so that I don't have to be told I don't look disabled. But that's wrong, because I shouldn't have to "look disabled" in order to be disabled. Just because I don't resemble society's vision of what someone with a disability should look like, it doesn't make me less disabled than I am or make me not disabled at all. I'm not going to change the way I look physically so that people can see I'm disabled, so what do I need to do in order to make people see that I am disabled?

At times, I do feel the need to carry some proof around with me so that, if people were ever to question my disability, I can just show them that. Then, whether I'm disabled or not won't be a question to be asked any more, as there will be literal proof that I do have cerebral palsy, which most people wouldn't be able to argue about. Let's face it, arguing against proof is like telling a brick wall to move, depending on the situation and what the proof is for. Feeling the need to carry proof around in order to prove to people that you're disabled, shouldn't be necessary in this day and age, or in any day and age actually. You wouldn't question whether someone has pink hair when they physically do have pink hair, so why question whether someone has a disability or not when they do have one?

I do get why people question some disabilities because certain disabilities are invisible, but as a society, we need to learn that not all disabilities are physical, some are invisible, and you can't always see them. In some cases, and luckily for me, it's a lot easier to prove that I'm disabled as my disability is a physical one. So my heart goes out to people all over the world who are living with invisible disabilities, who face being told (probably more than I do) that they don't look disabled. But whether disabilities are invisible or not, from my point of view it should never be questionable whether a person has one.

You could say I know what it's like having to prove to people who I am. It's so gut-wrenching at times, especially in situations such as when I'm parking outside a shop with members of my family. When I go to the shops, with my mum or whoever I'm with, we often park in a disabled space in the car park as it's easier for me to get to the shop from there. We often have a disabled badge as proof that we can do this and also people can verify that a disabled person has parked there and not just anyone — people who aren't disabled park in these spaces sometimes.

Most people are quite understanding about why we have parked there and don't have a problem with us doing so. However, in the past and still, to this day, there are people who have a problem with me and my mum (or whoever else I'm with) parking in disabled spaces. At times, we have been stared at in an unpleasant way, either when we're coming back to the car or when we're just getting out of the car. When this happens, I feel as if I need to act like I'm more disabled than I am, in order to make it more apparent to the people who give me evil looks that I'm disabled and need to park in a disabled space because of it. Yet again, I guess this all comes down to me "not looking disabled" because of the way I dress or something. Because I don't look it, it's as though my gait and how I walk due to my disability aren't enough proof for people to understand that I'm disabled.

It's not just evil looks I get when parking in a disabled space; there are also notes left on the windscreen or comments such as, "You shouldn't be parking there", or even the question, "Are you disabled?". Well, if I weren't disabled then I'm sure I wouldn't have a limp when I walk or a disabled badge as proof, and I probably wouldn't be parking in a disabled parking space, which anyone can see quite clearly.

I feel like saying this to people all the time, and to some, I may be seen as making a stupid comment and considered harsh and inconsiderate for not understanding why people ask questions like this, as well as for making the comment, and they may be right. But when you have a physical disability that's quite obvious, to spout questions like, "Are you disabled?" becomes irritating, especially when you get asked it quite a lot. We sometimes have to show people my disabled badge as another way of proving that we have the right to park there. I have had a negative reaction to our parking in a disabled space on many occasions. Why does this have to happen?

In society, I think, the image of how a disabled person should look like has been overtaken by the stereotypical vision I've mentioned several times in this chapter. Because of this, it's a shock for people when they see disabled people doing "normal" things and being "normal" human beings. But disabled people have the right to be like others, to wear stuff that's similar to stuff worn by others, and to do the same kinds of things that other people do.

Having said that, though, everyone is different, including people with disabilities: we each have different disabilities that affect us differently, or we might have the same disability as another, but individually it might affect us differently. I think this is also an issue: sometimes, disabled people are compared to one another and so, some expect all disabled people to look the same or to walk the same way or expect all disabled people to be in a wheelchair.

As someone who has lived with a disability all her life, I have found that disabled people are often expected to be in a wheelchair. Signs such as those found on the doors of disabled toilets, showing a person in a wheelchair, are often used as a sign for most things to do with disabilities. At the same time, I think that the sign showing a person in a wheelchair has brainwashed society into thinking that all disabled people are in wheelchairs, whereas this is not the case at all.

As I've said, disabilities can be physical, mental and also invisible — they can be a whole wide range of things. But people often associate disabilities, whether they're physical, mental or invisible, with that disabled sign, and so, when someone with a disability is told they don't look disabled, it's possibly down to society being used to thinking that disabled people should all be in wheelchairs. As this isn't always the case and not all disabled people are in wheelchairs, people are often quick to question whether a person has a disability or not, just because they're not in a wheelchair, taking their model from the disabled sign that is often seen in toilets and other places across the UK.

I'd like to think that, if signs, such as the one associated with disabilities which is often found on disabled toilet doors and in disabled parking spaces, were changed a bit to show that not every disability means being in a wheelchair, then maybe people's views on disabilities would change as well. I think that, if changes like this were to happen, people living with disabilities wouldn't have to feel the pressure of proving to people that they do have a disability and all disabilities would be seen as different, which is what they are.

Maybe, then, it would be seen as normal for a person like me, living with a disability, to wear makeup and be into the same fashions as others who may not necessarily be disabled. Maybe, then, there wouldn't be a stereotypical vision of what a disabled person should look like. I think that, in order to grow as a society and as a nation, we need to stop stereotyping things such as disabilities, so that the world can become more accepting and more understanding about things that have always lacked understanding. People don't have to look a certain way in order to be a certain something — the world doesn't work like that. Everyone's different, no one's the same, and so no one should be expected to look the same as another either, no matter who we are or what our circumstances might be.

Chapter Twenty-nine

Just Like You

People with disabilities are often labelled as "different" by many and this creates a negative image in people's minds when they think about disabilities. I can see how this might happen, as disability isn't a good thing, and in some cases, can be far from good — I know this from living with it my whole life. However, at the same time, in some people's eyes this negative image of disability doesn't always relate to the disability itself, it's also the people who are living with disabilities who are viewed negatively.

I've spoken a lot about how my individuality and who I am as a person have been affected by how others view me because I'm disabled. Often my disability comes first when people see me, and so my personality and everything else about me, apart from my disability, is overlooked by many people. Because of this, my life has been affected in so many ways: how I make friends; being written off as unable to do something before I've even tried to do it; how I'm seen by strangers; all of these are down to my disability, as are most things in my life. Because people have always seen my disability before seeing Issy and the person I am. I think they don't realise that I'm still a person — I still have hobbies and interests; I still have feelings just like everyone else; I still have dreams I wish to achieve in the future. I'm just like everyone else, and the same goes for everyone else out there living with disabilities all over the world — we're all still human. But it's as though, because we're disabled, all the other things in our lives are forgotten and don't really matter to anyone else.

For me, this has affected how I make friends and I think this is the most difficult aspect of all the things that my disability has disrupted. I've spoken about making friends previously and how difficult making friends and forming friendships have been for me, due to the fact that I'm disabled and how this is viewed in society. Again, when I've tried to make friends in the past, forming friendships like everyone else, my hobbies and all my other characteristics and interests are forgotten about. This creates a barrier for people who might get to know me as a friend, because my disability is the main reason why that barrier has been created and why people can't get past the barrier and see me for who I am.

All my life, I've been desperate to be accepted in society and to be seen in the same way as everyone else is seen. Because this hasn't exactly happened many times in my life, there have been moments when I have wondered why that is. When someone who doesn't have a disability meets someone else, it probably takes them a day or so to make friends with the other person. As for me, at times it has taken almost a year to make friends with someone who hasn't grown up with me and who doesn't know much about me or my disability.

Why is this? Why does it take the average, "normal" teenager a day or so to make a friend when it takes me nearly a year? It's because not being seen in the same way as everyone else creates the barrier I mentioned earlier between me and the rest of the world, you could say. That's the whole reason behind this, behind me doing something that takes far longer, but that's so easy for other people to do.

College was really hard in my first year, because of this and because of not being viewed in the same way as everyone else. I remember seeing a few girls in class who didn't know one another before starting college and who were complete strangers, then by lunchtime it seemed as though they were friends already and had been for years. Anyway, I thought, as they hadn't known one another that long, maybe they would be willing to include another person in their newly formed friendship group — me. So I asked if I could join them at lunchtime, as it was the first lunchtime at college for all of us, and I didn't have anyone to hang out with. I thought that, if these girls could make friends with one another within a couple of hours, then surely, it would be the same between me and them as well.

But it wasn't. It wasn't like that at all, which was quite disappointing for me, and my hope of making friends with them had been crushed. I've mentioned before how people act awkwardly around me most of the time, if I try to hang out with them, and this time it was exactly the same. I don't know why I thought it would be any different this time round, because it wasn't. Don't get me wrong, the girls weren't nasty in any way, they were actually quite genuine, but the barrier that's created by my disability got in the way, as it does most of the time.

But what got to me most of all was the fact that these girls were talking about different fashion brands they liked, which were the same fashion brands that I liked. As they were talking to one another about these fashion brands, I tried doing so too and attempted to join in the conversation they were having, because you could say we shared the same hobby of shopping for the same fashion brands. But it was as though they didn't want to include me in the conversation: after everything I said or tried saying in order to make conversation with them, it seemed they would shut me down by just giving one-word answers. There would be an awkward silence for a few seconds, and the girls would then carry on with their conversation.

This told me that it doesn't matter if I have the same interests as other people and other girls my age, that's not enough to break down the stigma through which disabled people are disqualified from being seen in the same way as everyone else, and in a way, are not part of society because of this. I've always wanted to feel I'm part of society and as though I'm being seen for who I am and not for my disability. It's been a big thing for me not to feel alien to the world, as I have felt many times, and to feel as though my disability can be overlooked by those around me, so that I wouldn't have to struggle with things that are easy for other people to do.

In some ways, I've always wished that I could have been born into a different generation and born as an adult, so that I wouldn't have to overcome the barriers and face the problems of growing up with a disability, not being able to make friends and never being seen as others are seen. Adulthood is where people have a better understanding of what disability is and I like to think that, because of this, the barriers that I had to face in my childhood wouldn't exist and it would be easier to make friends and do other social stuff as well. As stupid as it sounds, maybe being born as an adult — even though this is absolutely impossible — would've meant that I could live a life where I would be seen for the person I am. Maybe not, I don't know — this is just a crazy, slightly wacky wish that I make sometimes when life gets socially difficult for me.

I also wish that cerebral palsy and other disabilities that are out there could be seen as the norm in the world, so that they wouldn't be such an issue in society and people with all kinds of disabilities would feel part of the world and not left out of everything. I know what the opposite to this feels like, it's probably one of the loneliest feelings in the world, feeling like you don't belong anywhere in this life and that people see you only for your disability. If this were to change and people could see that disability is part of society as well and accept it more readily, then that feeling of loneliness I've felt on many occasions wouldn't be something that people like me would have to feel at all.

I like to think that, one day, just as I did on my first days at school and college, I will be able to walk into a room of complete strangers who don't know me and whom I don't know, and instead of my disability being the first thing these people see, for once they see my personality, my hobbies and interests, or even what I'm wearing or the colour of my hair — anything but my disability. Then I'll be seen for me, for the person I am, and not as this disabled girl any more; because even though my disability is a part of me, it's not all of me. There is so much more to me than just that.

It's been hard trying to get this across to everyone and for my disability not to be the first thing that's noticed when I meet new people. I guess all my life I've been trying to do that in order to achieve some sort of equality, so that people come to the realisation that I'm just like them and that my disability is just a minor aspect of who I am. I'm not my disability — which some people don't understand; but I'm hoping one day this can change and people will gain a better understanding of cerebral palsy and other disabilities too, so that equality between us will be a bigger factor than it is now and than it has been in the past.

I'm hoping that, as equality grows over time, people will realise that, although I have a disability, it doesn't define who I am in any way, shape or form; it doesn't control me or my life; it doesn't take over what I like doing; it doesn't change my personality or who I am as a person. Sure, it might make me different from others, and mean that I can't do things others can do, but deep down, I am just like any other seventeen-year-old girl my age and my disability shouldn't remove that fact. I may be different from others in this world in many ways, but at the same time, I am just like you.

Chapter Thirty

Finding Positivity in Disability

Disabilities are normally seen as negatives in today's world which, to be quite frank, they are. The way we see them and how they're viewed in society generally is usually in a negative way. Everything about disability and what it entails is viewed as negative. But what if that was all wrong? What if there are some aspects of having a disability that can be quite positive, and what if not everything that has to do with disability is negative?

As a society, I think we are quick to label everything that either is a disability or has something to do with disability as negative — all of it, we don't see anything about disability as positive in any way, shape or form. However, as a person who has lived with disability all her life, I have come to recognise the positives amongst all the negatives I've had to deal with and overcome as time has gone on.

For a long time, even I wasn't able see any positives in disability, and as someone living with it as well, I thought everything about being disabled was negative — there was nothing good about it. This way of thinking stuck with me for a long time and so, as I didn't see anything positive in being disabled, I didn't see any positives in the world around me either. In my eyes, the world was a horrible place for giving me a disability that gave me no purpose in life at all. During the time in which this thinking stuck with me, it began to affect my life as well and I didn't see anything positive, not just about my disability, but about myself either. I was living with a negative condition and so, as I saw it, I was negative as well. I can tell you that this didn't help me in any way at all. I was so angry with the world and I guess I surrounded myself with negativity, thinking that everything about my disability was horrible and that there was no beauty in it either.

This became the norm for me, thinking it was OK to despise myself and disqualifying myself when I couldn't do the simplest of things. I thought that hating myself and my disability was normal and that this was the way forward. I didn't even allow myself to try and find a single thing that might be positive about my disability. I didn't see that as an option. I didn't *want* to see it as an option, because I was so brainwashed into thinking it was totally normal to view myself in a negative light, and you could say that light wasn't a very bright one.

The best way in which I can describe this period in my life is to compare it to drawing the curtains, leaving the curtains drawn, and not even bothering to peep through them to see what was on the other side. Metaphorically, the curtains represented all the negativity that I had felt through the years about hating being disabled and having to deal with all the horrible stuff that came from this, including being bullied at school, being seen only for my disability, not being accepted by others, not accepting myself. All this meant that those curtains stayed firmly drawn in front of me.

On the side where I stood was the present I was living in, the past that I had lived, and all the negativity about my disability that surrounded me and had taken over my whole mind space. On the other side was my future and everything I had in front of me, which I couldn't quite see and refused to believe would happen. For a while, the curtains stayed drawn, and every now and then I would have a peep through them, but refused to open them more than that, because of the negativity that was eating away at me.

However, one day, I wanted to draw the curtains fully and see more of what was right in front of me, and get out of the darkness I was in. But then I figured that the only way I could do this would be to stop being so negative towards myself and my disability and to start looking for the positives instead. I didn't know exactly how I was going to do this, but I was so desperate to see the bigger picture in life that I was determined to do so

— no matter how hard it was going to be for me to draw those curtains.

Initially, in order to do this, I started to appreciate the smallest of things, whether it was the sun that was shining that day, or the people around me who loved and cared about me and who made me laugh, even down to appreciating the fact that I had got up that morning and was alive and breathing. I know that these things weren't positive in relation to my disability itself, but it was a start. The curtains were gradually opening more than they had opened in the past, and I finally got to see the positives around me instead of seeing the negativity and nothing else.

Even though, by this point, I didn't see anything positive about my disability yet, I wasn't in a place where I hated the world as much and didn't want to be in it, because counting all the positive things in my life, such as being alive and all the other simple things that were positive, made a difference to how I viewed the world. The anger inside me that I felt towards the world for giving me this disability was gradually becoming less and less, and it slowly went away and turned into happiness and appreciation for the life that I was living.

At this point, my view of the future got a little brighter and I saw what I had in front of me which, in the past, I had blocked out and didn't want to think about because of all the negativity I was feeling at that stage in my life. This didn't happen overnight — I didn't just wake up one day, after years of feeling anger towards the world and then that anger disappeared and life automatically became positive and great, it wasn't like that at all. The feelings of positivity came over time and not within a day or two, but even though it took a long time for me to see these feelings, they came.

Soon, at a time when I had been counting all the simplest things in my life that made it positive and that weren't to do with my disability, I started to see the positives in my disability as well as in the things around me. A disability is generally a negative thing, so this was hard to do. To begin with, instead of trying to find the positives in my disability itself, I started to look for all the good things in myself, the aspects of me that I liked and found positive.

Initially, it was as simple as finding my sea-blue eyes really cool and pretty, you could say — it wasn't a massive thing that a person could like about themselves, but it was something I liked about myself, and that was better than nothing. After realising that my eyes were an attribute of my physical appearance that I liked, I then started to like my blonde hair and the colour of it. Then it was my clothes and the fashions that I wore — in which I may be a bit biased as this was the fashion look that I liked and was into and so, of course, I was bound to like it. I liked it on me and how I looked in it.

I soon saw more and more positive things about myself, and then this turned into finding positive things about my disability. These included my empathetic personality, because, in my eyes, my disability has made me understand the needs of others and what they might be going through, just as I've been through so much in my life due to being disabled. Therefore, I could understand what it was like for people who were going through a lot and could relate to their experiences; I would add, without blowing my own trumpet too much, that I am a kind person because of my circumstances. Another positive was the fact that, even though I was disabled, it didn't get in the way of me walking and talking and doing things, and this made me appreciate my life a bit more. Once upon a time, my disability might have meant that I wouldn't be able to walk or talk and wouldn't be able to do anything at all.

There were loads of other things, apart from these two things, that I saw as positive in regard to my disability. They included being able to educate others on disabilities, which, I have found, is a topic that's not really talked about; meeting people I wouldn't have met if I hadn't been disabled, and who have had a positive impact on my life; doing really well in my life in relation to my disability and learning how to handle it. All these things, which I found quite positive in relation to my disability, made my life brighter in many ways and soon, those curtains had opened fully and I didn't see my disability as such a negative thing any more.

Maybe if disability wasn't seen as such a negative thing in the world and instead was seen as part of it and celebrated as an aspect of society, I think people living with disabilities everywhere wouldn't see it as a negative thing like I did and would feel better about being disabled. I still see negative things about my disability, but I also see positive things about it as well. It was hard for me to recognise what was positive about being disabled, but now I have done this I can see the bigger picture in life and the beauty within it, and that includes my disability as well.

Chapter Thirty-one

Dear Cerebral Palsy...

The pain up the backside that has been with me right from birth, my worst enemy, everything that I hate: living with you these past few years has been a whirlwind, and to be honest, I don't really know whether I hate you or not. What I have to say may sound a bit confusing to some, but I am saying it because you're something that restricts me from doing things. The truth is — and I'm sure that if you were a real person you'd agree — that you want to be in control of my body and don't want me to be able-bodied at all.

If it were down to you, I would be in a wheelchair right now. Not only do you try to restrict me but you're a barrier too, a metaphorical wall that gets in front of me, especially when I meet new people, because you want all the attention to be on yourself instead of me. When we do meet new people together, you want to be seen before I am and you want people to realise that you are there, so I guess, borderline, you're an attention seeker as well as a pain in the backside. You also make it harder for me to live a perfectly normal life in which I can do whatever I want to do and be free, without you trying to bring me down and making it a struggle for me to do things. Every ache and pain that I experience is a sign of you showing you want control over my life, and every time I feel those aches and pains, they're a sign telling me that, no matter where I am in life, no matter what I do or where I go, you will unfortunately be with me and walking beside me every step of the way — sometimes even trying to trip me up when you want me to let you win and take over my body.

Alternatively, however, even though you are my worst enemy, at the same time you're like a companion as well, something that will never leave my side, no matter what. This sounds crazy but let me explain. Throughout my life with you, cerebral palsy, you have shown me beauty in the simplest things; these are things that most people take for granted and that you hate me appreciating, because it shows that I'm winning the battle we've been fighting for years now. But even though you don't want me doing normal activities that everyone else can do easily, you've allowed me to win and do them, so that I can have a chance of experiencing doing such simple things. You see, if I didn't have you beside me, I could easily have taken those things for granted and not really thought much about them, just like everyone else does on a daily basis. But because I've had to fight against you to be able to do those little things, I don't take them for granted, because I feel incredibly lucky that you let me win when I was fighting you to be able to achieve them. And so I thank you for allowing me to be the person I've always wanted to be and for giving me the independence to do that, when you didn't really want to let that happen.

You see, cerebral palsy, we're complete opposites but identical at the same time. All the time we're fighting each other: when I want one thing, you want the opposite; when I succeed, you absolutely hate it; and when you succeed, I absolutely hate it. I guess that makes us complete opposites because we don't want the same thing, and we never have from the day we first met. But what makes us identical is that we both know what it's like desperately fighting for what we want, we both know the pain we feel when we don't succeed, even after trying our best. We know what it's like living with barriers and how frustrating it can be when we can't get through them, so I guess we can relate to each another when we come face to face with all these things. Even though we hate what each of us can do, we both know the feelings we have when we struggle and what it's like to go through these exact same feelings all the time for the same reasons.

I've always wanted to ask you a load of questions and I know that you won't be able to answer them because you're not a real person. But here's one, or maybe a few, of the questions I've always wanted to ask you. Why me? Why did you have to choose me to be the person whose body you live in and try to control every day? I don't get why I was one of many people out there whom you have chosen to try and control, and I will never get why I have to be one of those people; but then I guess you had to choose someone and that someone was me. Even though I don't know why you chose me, I have an idea, and maybe the idea is that you knew you wouldn't get an easy fight with me, that I haven't given in, and to this day, will never give in to you and let you win. If I had done that, I wouldn't have had such a fulfilling life as I have enjoyed so far. I wouldn't have achieved what I have done.

Sometimes, you make me want to give up on life as well as on cerebral palsy and you make me question my worth. I sometimes wonder: Does living with you mean that I'm not going to get the life I want to live? Does it mean that I'll live a completely different life from my dream life? Do you have a different plan for me? You anger me: Why, amongst everyone I know, do I have to be the one who's different, who is seen as different and who will always be seen as different by other people? Sometimes, I want to punch you in the face for doing this to me and making my life much harder than it might have been. But here's the thing — I can't because you're not an actual person, which means you don't have a face to punch, unfortunately. At other times I just ignore you and try to forget that you are there.

Ignoring you and being angry with you isn't going to get me very far, though. It will just make me feel bad about myself and make you feel powerful because you've got what you wanted, which is me being angry and annoyed, not just with you, cerebral palsy, but with the world too for making me this way. I don't want that. I don't want you getting your own way and defeating me. So instead of being angry with you, I choose to embrace you, to be proud of you because, as crazy as it sounds, without you I wouldn't be the person I am today. You have made me even more resilient because I've had to deal with you for so long, I am stronger because, through every fight between us in which you've tried to bring me down and make me give up, most of the time I have defeated you and won. I am thankful to have a life because I know that it was almost taken from me by you, but now that I have been able to keep it, I realise how precious life can be and that every second counts. So for that, thank you, cerebral palsy. Thank you for making me realise all this and for making me realise that, in order to be me, I need you. So, let's look forward to the future together.

Epilogue

I am

I am beautiful.
I am powerful.
I am not broken.
I am strong.
I am kind.
I am not defined.
I am not my disability.
I am me.